# Your Body
# and
# How It Works

written by Ovid K. Wong, Ph.D.
illustrations by Lindaanne Donohoe
anatomical photographs by
Lester V. Bergman & Associates, Inc.

CHILDRENS PRESS ®

CHICAGO

This book is dedicated to two eager learners—my children,
JONATHAN & NATHANIEL

Library of Congress Cataloging-in-Publication Data

Wong, Ovid K.
   Your body and how it works.
   Includes index.
   Summary: Introduces the workings of the human body, system by system, with related activities and thought questions.
   1. Human physiology—Juvenile literature.   2. Body, Human—Juvenile literature.   3. Human physiology—Experiments—Juvenile literature.
   [1. Human physiology.   2. Body, Human]
   I. Title.
   QP37.W66 1986        612        86-9689
   ISBN 0-516-00534-0

## PICTURE ACKNOWLEDGMENTS

### PHOTOGRAPHS
Photographs not listed below were supplied by Lester V. Bergman & Associates, Inc.
Nawrocki Stock Photo: © Jim Whitmer—8

### ILLUSTRATIONS
Illustrations not listed below were supplied by Lindaanne Donohoe
Phyllis Adler—11
Lester V. Bergman & Associates, Inc.—34, 97, 98, 109

# TABLE OF CONTENTS

## Sources of Materials

Most of the materials used in this book may be purchased from your local hardware store or supermarket. However, materials may be ordered from the following sources:

Carolina Biological Supply Company
Burlington, North Carolina 27215
(800) 632-1231

Delta Education
P.O. Box M
Nashua, New Hampshire 03061-6012
(800) 258-1302

Fisher Scientific Company
4901 W. LeMoyne Street
Chicago, Illinois 60651
(800) 621-4769

NASCO West Inc.
P.O. Box 3837
Modesto, California 95352
(209) 529-6957

# Preface

*Man wonders over the restless sea*
*the flowing water and the sight of the sky*
*And forgets that of all wonders*
*Man himself is the most wonderful.*
  St. Augustine, Fourth Century A.D.

For centuries people have dreamed of building a perfect machine. This ideal machine would be able to work continuously, with minimal repair and maintenance. One scientist long ago built a machine that was run by flowing water. He called it the perpetual moving machine. Unfortunately, his invention eventually stopped due to the resistant forces of gravity and friction. Since then scientists have built countless machines. These are all wonderful machines, but none can match the supermachine that we are going to study.

This supermachine is very complex. Its motor may run for seventy or more years without stopping. It is self-servicing, self-oiling, self-cooling, and self-warming. It has its own spare parts and many safety devices. Amazingly, some of its parts become stronger as they are used. The machine also has the ability to store millions of facts for later use. What is this machine? A computer? A car? No! It is your own body.

Each chapter of this book has some information about the body. This information is followed by a series of practical activities— and a few surprises too. So get ready for an adventure. You are about to discover and explore the real you!

# Introduction

A very special kind of animal inhabits the planet Earth. It lives in a wide geographical area, as far north as the Arctic and as far south as the Antarctic. It lives at altitudes that vary from sea level to high mountain-top level. Like other animals, this one is made up of cells, tissues, organs, and systems. To stay alive this animal must have a continuous supply of air, water, and food. One thing sets it apart from all other animals—its ability to communicate and think. This animal is you—the human.

The human is a very complicated machine with many parts and systems. Some systems of the human body might be compared with the systems of a car. The spark plugs, coil, distributor, and battery will not work until they are put together in an electrical system. Furthermore, other systems such as the motor, steering, cooling, suspension, braking, and fuel systems have to work together to make the car run. In much the same way, the human systems made of cells, tissues, and organs have to work together to carry on important life activities. There are ten major systems in your body:

**Key Terms**
- cell
- organ
- system
- tissue

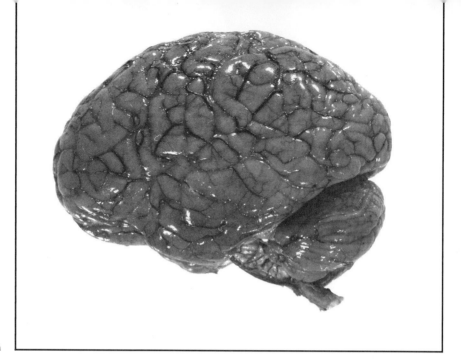

Human brain

**THE COVERING SYSTEM.** The skin, along with the hair and nails, forms the body surface. The skin protects the body from its environment.

**THE SUPPORTIVE SYSTEM.** The bones support and protect some soft parts of the body. The inside of the bone—the bone marrow—has the important job of making new blood cells.

**THE MUSCULAR SYSTEM.** The muscles move the body—the arms, the legs, and the head. You smile and frown by moving your face muscles.

**THE CIRCULATORY SYSTEM.** The heart and blood vessels make up the circulatory system, which moves absorbed food and oxygen through the body. It also removes soluble wastes.

**THE BREATHING SYSTEM.** The lungs and the air passages in this system permit the gaseous exchange vital to all life activities.

**THE DIGESTIVE SYSTEM.** This system involves the entire food passage and includes the various digestive organs, such as the stomach and the intestines. The system breaks down food materials so that they can be used by the body.

**THE WASTE-DISPOSAL SYSTEM.** The kidneys remove dissolved wastes. The skin and the lungs are included as parts of this system because they too remove forms of bodily waste.

**THE HORMONAL SYSTEM.** This system includes a number of glands and the special chemicals, called hormones, that they produce. Hormones regulate many activities in your body. For example, how fast you grow is regulated by a hormone produced by a gland in your head.

**THE NERVOUS SYSTEM.** The brain and nerves make up this system, which enables you to respond to changes around you. Some nerve cells tell you that the weather is very cold; other nerve cells then tell you to put on more clothes.

**THE REPRODUCTIVE SYSTEM.** This system is made up of a group of organs that have the ability to produce a new human being. This ability to reproduce keeps the human race from dying off and disappearing from the earth.

## How Is Your Body Like a Machine?

### Materials
none needed

### Procedure
1. Look around you to find some machines with motors and moving parts. They might be machines such as a motor car, a sewing machine, a washing machine, a lawn mower, and a vacuum cleaner. Any motorized toy, such as a car, a truck, a train, or a robot is fine if the big machines are not available.
2. Select 4 machines and label them A, B, C, and D. Then answer the questions below. You may ask your parents or teachers to help you if you are not familiar with some of the machines being discussed.
   a. How old is the machine?
   b. Does the machine work 24 hours a day?
   c. How often does it need repair maintenance?
3. Answer the same questions about yourself, assuming that you are also a "machine."
4. Compare and contrast the answers you gave for questions a, b, and c in items 3 and 4.

### Conclusions
1. The human is like a machine in many ways.
2. The human "machine" works much harder (24 hours a day) than other machines. The human "machine" is usually self-repairing, whereas a car, lawn mower, or motorized toy is not.

## Think and Explore

1. Which of the machines that you selected is the most durable? Why?
2. How does the durable machine that you selected compare with the human "machine"?
3. How is your body like a machine?
4. How is your body not like a machine?

# What Are the Different Systems of Your Body?

## Materials

old books and magazines
scissors
glue
poster board

## Procedure

1. Cut pictures from magazines that show different body systems at work. For example, a weight lifter could be used to show the use of the muscles; a person eating might illustrate digestion. Identify as many different systems at work as possible.
2. Glue the pictures onto a sheet of poster board.

## Conclusion

There are ten major systems in the body. These are the covering, supportive, muscular, circulatory, breathing, digestive, waste-disposal, hormonal, nervous, and reproductive systems.

## Think and Explore

1. Which body system is the most important? Why?
2. Which body system is the most important for growth?
3. Can a body system work all by itself? Explain.

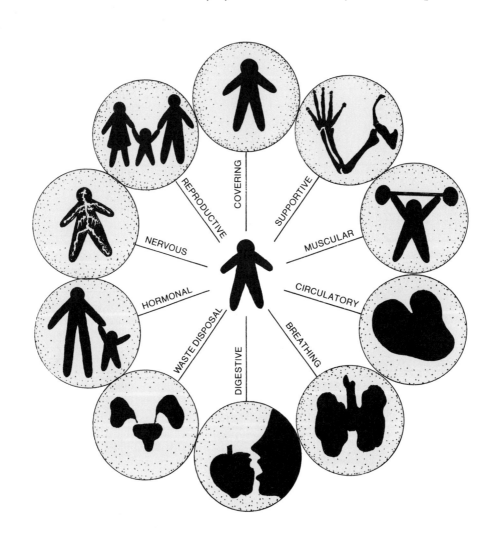

# Chapter 1

# The Covering System

The covering system of your body is the skin. It covers your whole body like a piece of tight wrapping. Because of its large surface area, the skin is considered the largest organ of the body. It has two main layers. The outer layer is made up of dead cells that are regularly replaced by dividing cells that are pushing up from below. The inner layer contains live cells with blood vessels, nerves, and other tissues.

Skin color is created by the amount of activity of a group of special cells under the outer layer. The activity of these cells is affected by factors such as sunlight and by traits inherited from parents. Exposure to sunlight produces suntan and freckles in some people. Skin color of people of different races is produced by the skin color trait of their parents, their grandparents, and their great-grandparents.

Nails and hair are outgrowths of the skin. Oil from the oil gland serves to moisten the hair and smooth the skin. Nails and hair have no nerve supply. This is why cutting the hair or nails causes no pain.

The skin does many important jobs. These include protecting the body from bacteria, preventing the body from becoming dried out, controlling the body temperature so that the body doesn't get too warm or cold, and telling the body about its surroundings through the senses of touch, pain, heat, and cold.

It is important to take care of the skin. Keep it clean by bathing regularly. Clean and cover any open wound immediately. Be careful of too much sun. It

**Key Terms**
- bacteria
- cancer
- nerve
- organ
- sweat
- sweat gland
- sweat pore
- trait

may be true that you look good with a suntan. However, we know that overexposure to the sun can be harmful and can cause the skin cells to reproduce abnormally. The condition that results is skin cancer.

## Facts
- In an adult, the total area of the skin is more than 18 square feet (about 1.67 square meters).
- In an adult, the skin weighs about 6 pounds (2.7 kilograms).
- The hair in a man's beard is about as tough as copper wire of the same thickness.
- Every person's fingerprints are unique. No two people—not even identical twins—have the same fingerprints.

Hair follicle, scalp

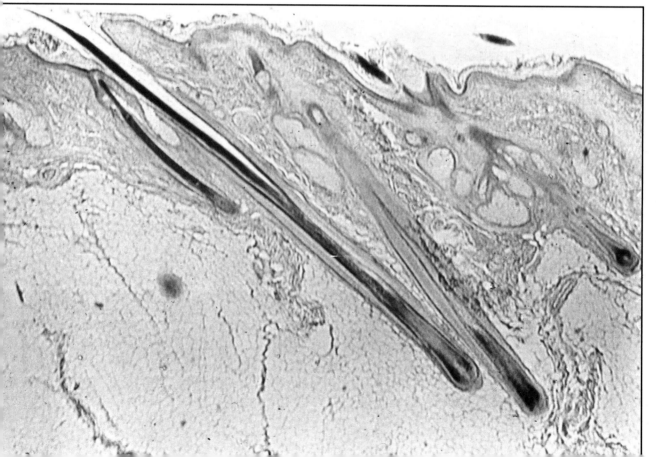

# Where Are Your Senses of Temperature?

## Materials
ballpoint pen
ruler
2 metal rods
   (for example, knitting needles)
2 glass containers

ice water
hot water
thin bristle (hair from a paintbrush)
paper and pencil
thermometer

## Procedure
Do this activity with a partner.

1. Ask your partner to blindfold you. Your partner is the tester; you are the subject. The rest of the directions are for the tester.

2. Draw a square (2 centimeters [about 1 inch] on each side) on the upper surface of the subject's forearm, using the ballpoint pen and the ruler.

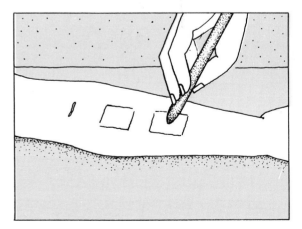

3. Fill one of the glass containers with ice water. Fill the other with hot (but not boiling) water. The hot water should be about 45° Centigrade (113° Fahrenheit). Use the thermometer to help you to find out the temperature of the water. Put one metal rod in the ice water, the other in the hot water.

4. Ask the subject to close his or her eyes. Use the ice-cold metal rod (from the ice-water container) to touch different points in the 2-centimeter square. Make sure the rod taken from the water is wiped dry. When the subject feels the cold sensation, mark the point with a dark dot.
5. Repeat step 4 with the metal rod taken from the hot-water container. Make sure the rod is wiped dry. When the subject feels the warm sensation, mark the point with a circle.
6. Use a thin bristle to touch different points in the square. When the subject feels the touch sensation, mark the point with a small x.
7. Redraw the 2-centimeter square on a piece of paper. Examine the different places where dark dots, open circles, and x's appear. Can you see any pattern of dots, circles, and x's?

## Conclusions
1. The sensations of cold, warmth, and touch are located separately and independently in your skin. The sensations are clustered in groups on the skin.
2. The nerves that give you the touch and temperature sensations are different. In other words, there is one nerve receptor for cold, one for warmth, and another one for touch.

## Think and Explore
1. Do you think pain is related to touch? To pressure? To temperature?
2. Put your hand first in hot (not boiling) water and then in warm water. The hand that was in warm water after being in hot water feels cold. Why?
3. Which part of your skin is more sensitive to changes in temperature? Why?

# How Can You Test Your Sense of Touch?

## Materials
cardboard
straight pins
blindfold (handkerchief or scarf, for example)
paper and pencil

## Procedure
Do this activity with a partner.
1. Prepare five pin boards by pushing pins through pieces of cardboard as shown in the diagram.
2. Ask your partner to blindfold you. Your partner is the tester; you are the subject.
3. Have the tester touch your fingertip with the five pin boards one after another in mixed order.
4. Each time, tell whether you feel one pinpoint or two pinpoints. The tester is to record the correct answer and your answer without saying anything.
5. Record the results on the first line of the table on page 20. For each correct answer, mark an *x* in the space. If you had a wrong answer, leave the space blank.

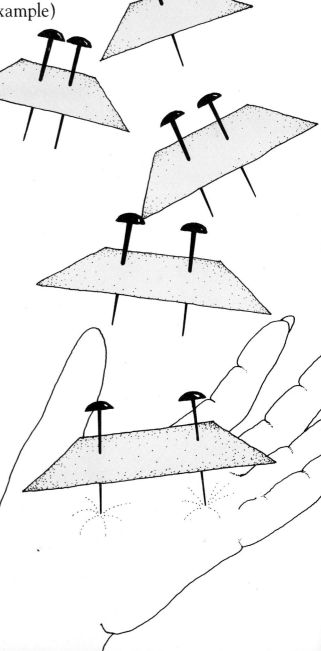

### Table of Responses

| Distance between pinpoints | 0 in. (0 pin) | ¼ in. (.6 cm.) | ½ in. (1.3 cm.) | 1 in. (2.5 cm.) | 2 in. (5 cm.) |
|---|---|---|---|---|---|
| fingertip | _____ | _____ | _____ | _____ | _____ |
| palm of hand | _____ | _____ | _____ | _____ | _____ |
| back of hand | _____ | _____ | _____ | _____ | _____ |
| inside of forearm | _____ | _____ | _____ | _____ | _____ |
| outside of forearm | _____ | _____ | _____ | _____ | _____ |

6. In the same way, test the other areas of the skin listed in the table and record the results.

## Conclusions
1. Some areas of your skin are more sensitive to touch than are others.
2. The areas that are most sensitive to touch are your fingertips.

## Think and Explore
1. Examine the completed table from the experiment. List in order the areas of your skin from the most sensitive to touch to the least sensitive.
2. Is it important that some areas of your skin are more sensitive to touch? Why?

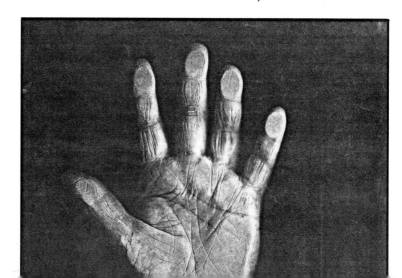

## *How Is Fingerprinting Your Body's Signature?*

### Materials
clean glass (glass slide or water glass)
white powder, such as baby powder
carbon paper (nonsmudge carbon paper won't work)
 or an inked stamp pad
white paper
magnifying glass

### Procedure
1. Press your fingertip on the glass.
2. Sprinkle the powder on the glass surface. Blow off the excess powder.
3. Hold the glass against a light to see the print.
4. Press your fingertip on a piece of carbon paper or an inked stamp pad.
5. Press the inked finger lightly on a piece of white paper.
6. Examine the fingerprint carefully with a magnifying glass.
7. Repeat steps 4, 5, and 6 with the other fingers.
8. Use the diagram to help you identify the major parts of fingerprints—arch, loop, and whorl.

### Conclusions
1. There are different ways to see fingerprints. Sprinkling powder on a print is one method. Making a print with carbon paper is another.
2. No two fingerprints are the same. Even your own ten fingerprints are all different. Because fingerprints are all different, they provide good clues for police work. Leaving your fingerprint may be as good as leaving your name and address.

## Think and Explore

1. Do you think fingerprints can be changed? Explain your answer.
2. Do fingerprints change if a person cuts a finger and the skin grows back on?
3. Do you think everybody should be required to have his or her fingerprints on record with the police department? Explain.

## Where Can You Find the Sweat Pores of Your Skin?

### Materials
shallow container
water
cornstarch
absorbent paper
      (for example, paper towel)
scissors
iodine

### Procedure

1. In the shallow container, prepare a cornstarch solution of two teaspoons of cornstarch mixed with one-half cup of water. Stir the solution well.
2. Prepare the sweat-pore test paper. Cut up small pieces of absorbent paper and dip the paper in the cornstarch solution. Let the paper dry completely.
3. Paint both the back of your hand and your palm with iodine. Let the iodine dry on your skin.
4. Work up a sweat by doing some exercise. Push-ups and running in place are good exercises for working up a sweat.

5. Press the test paper to the back and palm of your hand immediately after exercising. Examine the paper carefully. What do you see?

## Conclusion

The sweat activates the iodine and starch solution to produce a dark color. The location of the sweat pores shows up as dark spots on the test paper.

## Think and Explore

1. There are about 2 million sweat pores in your skin. The pores are connected to sweat-producing glands called sweat glands. There are more sweat pores in certain skin areas. Can you tell from the experiment whether you have more sweat pores in your palm or on the back of your hand?
2. Will the same experiment help you to locate the other sweat pores of your body? Support your answer with specific examples.
3. How does the skin cool the body by sweating?
4. How does regular bathing help to keep the skin healthy? Why?

## Do Sunscreens Prevent Sunburn?

### Materials
sunscreen lotion #4, #8, and #15

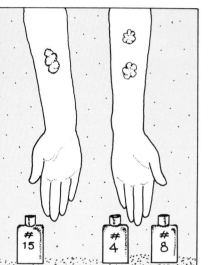

### Procedure
1. Rub a drop of #4 sunscreen lotion on the underside of your left forearm, covering a spot about half the size of a dime.
2. Rub the same size drop of #8 sunscreen lotion about 3 inches (7.6 centimeters) from the #4 lotion.
3. On your right arm cover the same size area with the #15 lotion.
4. Go out into strong sunlight for about 45 minutes, keeping your forearms turned up to the sun.
5. The following day compare the differences in the three spots.

### Conclusion
The three spots are different shades. These results are seen clearly only when the arms have been exposed to really strong sunlight.

### Think and Explore
1. How are the effects of the sunscreen lotion different? How do the lotions vary in their ability to protect the skin from the sun?
2. Which sunscreen lotion should you use on your first trip to a sunny beach in the summer? Why?
3. What helps you to decide which sunscreen products to buy?

# Where Are the Wear Areas of Your Skin?

## Materials
tincture of iodine
cotton swab

## Procedure

1. Apply a drop of tincture of iodine on the palm of your hand using a cotton swab. Allow it to dry.
2. Do the same thing to the back of your hand, the tip of your finger, and the inside of your arm near the elbow.
3. Check the spots regularly over a two-week period. Make careful observations and draw some conclusions from them.

## Conclusion
The color of the spots indicates the degree of wear of the skin area. Normally the finger and hand are both used and washed more than the inside of your arm.

## Think and Explore
1. What happens to the skin that is worn away?
2. How does the skin repair itself?
3. Is it possible to transplant a piece of skin from one person to another? Why?

# Chapter 2

# The Supportive System

**Key Terms**
- anti-invasion factor
- calcium
- cartilage
- centigrade
- joint
- lung
- marrow
- measurement
- phosphorus
- plaque
- skeleton
- vinegar
- vitamin

The bones are the body's supportive system. They are generally divided into two major groups: (1) bones of the middle part, including the skull, backbone, and ribs; and (2) bones of the arms and legs, including the shoulder and hip bones. Look at the photograph. How many bones do you recognize?

The supportive system of the body is like the framework of a building. It gives shape and support. However, the skeleton is also different from the framework of a building. The framework of a building cannot move, but the skeleton, along with the muscles, can. The place where two or more bones are joined together is called a joint. Most joints in the body (for example, elbow, knee, and ankle) allow the body to move. Pay attention to your breathing. Put your hands on your ribs. Can you feel your ribs moving up and down? The ribs move up and out when the air you breathe in expands your lungs. They move down and in when you exhale. Move your arm around. In how many different directions can you move it? Your arm can move in many directions.

When you were born, your skeleton was made of soft bones called cartilage. When you grow up, your body still has cartilage. Feel the tips of your nose and ears. They are made of cartilage. Cartilage is important in other places in the body. There are pads of cartilage between sections of the backbone. The pads prevent the bones from rubbing against each other and the nerves. They act as cushions.

Some parts of the skeleton do more than support the body. They protect some of its soft parts. For example, the skull protects the brain, and the ribs protect the heart and lungs. Do you see any similarity between the eggshell, which protects the egg yolk, and the skull, which protects the brain?

The bones have two other important jobs. Have you ever looked at a section of a beef or pork bone? In the center of the bone is a soft, red material called the bone marrow. The bone marrow has the important job of making new blood cells. Also, your body needs important minerals called calcium and phosphorus for many activities. The bones store these minerals.

The supportive system of the body—the skeleton—does a number of important jobs: (1) it gives shape and support to the body, (2) it protects soft parts, such as the brain and lungs, and cushions others, (3) it makes blood cells, (4) it stores minerals, and (5) it assists in movement.

## Facts

- Babies are born with about 350 separate bones.
- A full-grown person has about 206 bones.
- One quarter of the bones in an adult skeleton are found in the foot.
- The largest bone in your body is the thighbone. The smallest is the middle-ear bone.
- Scientists have found that the cartilage contains a special substance called anti-invasion factor (AIF). In the laboratory AIF has been shown to slow down cancer and some gum diseases.

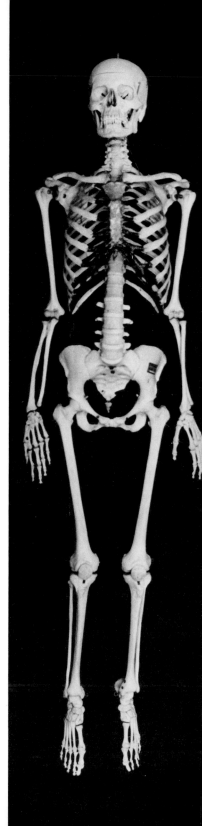

# How True Is the Expression "Dry as a Bone"?

## Materials
large beef or pork bone
weighing scale

## Procedure
1. Obtain a large beef or pork bone from the meat department where you shop.
2. Weigh the bone on the scale and record the weight in pounds and/or ounces (kilograms and/or grams).
3. Heat the bone in an oven at 150°F (65°C) for 4 hours.
4. Remove the bone from the oven and allow it to cool completely.
5. Determine the weight of the bone again.
6. Compare the weights of the bone before and after heating. What do you find?

## Conclusions
1. The weight of the bone is less after heating because water evaporated from the bone.
2. The weight composition of a bone is about 25 percent water.

## Think and Explore
1. How do you prove that water is a part of the bone?
2. A dry bone weighs 70 pounds. How much did the bone weigh when it was fresh? Explain how you determined this weight.

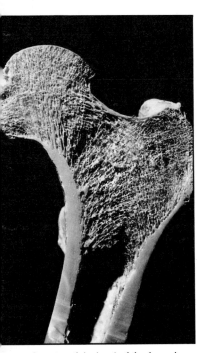

Interior of the head of the femur bone

# What Happens When Minerals Are Removed from Bones?

## Materials
leg or thighbone from uncooked chicken
paper towel
jar
vinegar

## Procedure
1. Remove all meat from the chicken bone. Wash the bone and dry it with a paper towel.
2. Feel the bone. Try to bend it gently. Record what happens.
3. Fill the jar with vinegar. Put the bone in the vinegar for one week.
4. Remove the bone from the vinegar at the end of a week. Wash the bone and dry it with a paper towel.
5. Feel the bone. Try to bend it gently. Record what happens.
6. Compare your notes for steps 2 and 5. How do they compare?

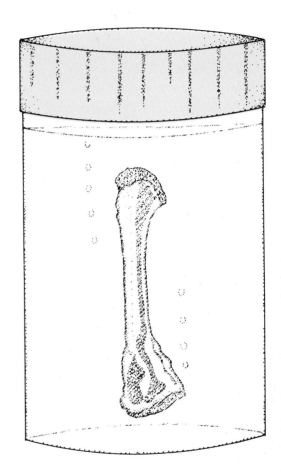

## Conclusions
1. The bone feels hard and cannot be bent before it is in the vinegar.
2. The bone feels soft and can be bent easily after it has been soaked in vinegar. Vinegar is a mild acid. It removes minerals from the bone, thus making it weak and soft.

### Think and Explore

1. If you did not eat foods containing minerals, how would your bones be affected?
2. How would a lack of minerals affect the ability of your skeleton to support your body?
3. Vitamin D is needed to help build strong bones and teeth. Why is this vitamin often called the sunshine vitamin?

## How Can You Reduce Plaque on Teeth?

### Materials
toothbrush
toothpaste
plaque-disclosing tablet (available in local drugstores)

### Procedure

1. Brush teeth in the left half of the mouth using the up-and-down method for 5 minutes after each meal.
2. Brush teeth in the right half of the mouth using the side-to-side method for 5 minutes after each meal.
3. Repeat steps 1 and 2 for two weeks.
4. Put a plaque-disclosing tablet in your mouth and let it dissolve.
5. Look in the mirror to compare the plaque areas in the mouth. Which side has more plaque?

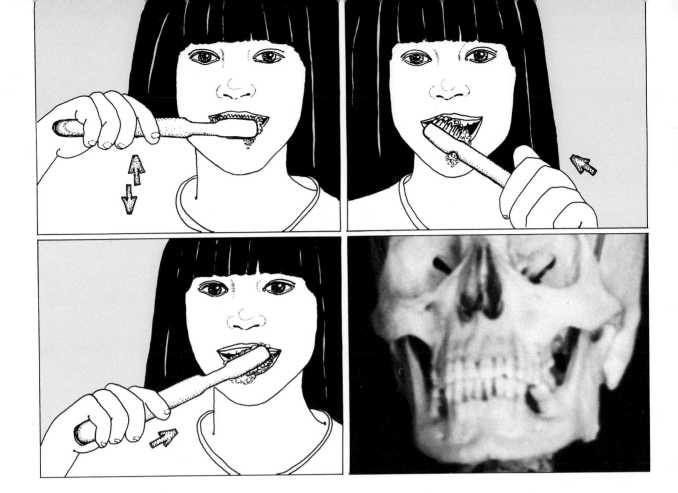

## Conclusions

1. The plaque areas on the teeth are colored by the disclosing tablet.
2. The left side of the mouth has less plaque.
3. The up-and-down method of brushing teeth is more effective in reducing plaque.

## Think and Explore

1. Are teeth a part of the skeleton or the digestive system? Explain.
2. Can brushing alone prevent bad breath? Why?
3. What are some of the ways that teeth are lost or can be damaged?
4. Count the number of teeth you have.

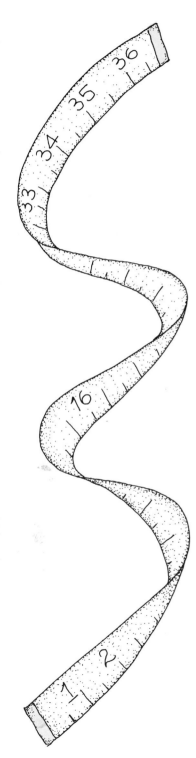

# Can You Change Your Height Overnight?

## Materials
measuring tape

## Procedure
1. Measure the height of your body at different times of the day. Take the first measurement when you get up in the morning. Take the second one in the afternoon, about lunchtime. Take the third one before you go to bed. Record each measurement.
2. Compare the three measurements.
3. Repeat steps 1 and 2 for further measurement comparison.

## Conclusion
There are small differences in the three measurements. The first measurement is the tallest. The last measurement is the shortest. The morning measurement is the tallest because the cartilage in the backbone is least compressed after hours of sleep. The measurement in the evening is the shortest because cartilage in the backbone is compressed by the weight of the body for the whole day.

## Think and Explore
1. What are some of the factors that affect growth?
2. Look at the photograph of the skeleton (page 27). Which bones are affected most by growth?

# Chapter 3

# The Muscular System

The muscles in your body make up the muscular system. You have more than 600 muscles in your body. They can be divided into two groups according to how they are controlled. You can control muscles that help you to sit, walk, run, and throw a ball. You tell them what to do and when to do it. These muscles, such as the arm and leg muscles, are in the group called voluntary muscles. Do you have to think about moving your heart muscle every moment of your life? No, because the action of the heart muscle is not controlled by your will and mind. Muscles of the heart, blood vessels, and stomach are in the group called involuntary muscles. A few muscles—those that control breathing and the eyelids—are both voluntary and involuntary.

The muscles are connected to the bones by tough tissues called tendons. You can feel the tendons in your hand and wrist. Try to feel the big tendon that connects the large calf muscle of your leg to the heel.

Muscles move by contraction and relaxation. Let us examine the upper arm muscle called the biceps. Contraction pulls the biceps to make it short and thick. Relaxation returns the biceps to its original shape, long and thin. Most muscles that move bones work in pairs. One muscle pulls a bone in one direction. The other muscle of the pair pulls the bone in the opposite direction. Remember, muscles can only pull. They cannot push. Therefore, to move a bone one muscle contracts (pulls) while the other muscle of the pair relaxes.

**Key Terms**
- biceps
- contraction of muscle
- involuntary
- meat grain
- relaxation of muscle
- tendon
- triceps
- voluntary

Soft, flabby muscles are out-of-shape muscles. Proper exercise and a balanced diet make the muscles strong and firm.

## Facts
- The largest muscle of the body is the muscle that you sit on. The smallest is in the middle ear.
- You have more than 35 face muscles to help you to express yourself.
- Activities of most muscles are started by the brain.
- Even when the body is relaxed, muscles still pull somewhat to maintain muscle tone.

Muscles of the leg and buttocks

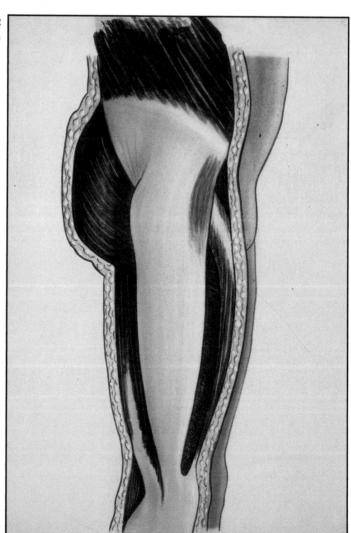

# How Do Muscles Work in Pairs?

## Materials
none needed

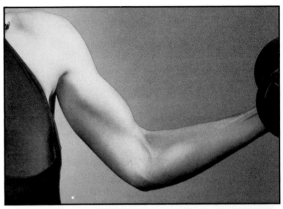

## Procedure
1. Roll up your sleeve to expose your upper arm.
2. Locate the biceps and triceps muscles. The biceps is on the front of the upper arm. The triceps is located on the back of the upper arm.
3. Place the elbow on a tabletop. Feel the biceps and triceps as you raise and lower your forearm.
4. Answer these questions:
   How do the two muscles act to raise the forearm?
   Which muscle contracts?
   Which muscle relaxes?

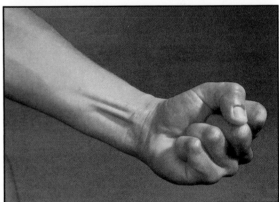

Arm muscles (top) and wrist tendons (above)

## Conclusions
1. When the forearm is raised, the biceps contracts (pulls) and the triceps relaxes.
2. When the forearm is lowered, the biceps relaxes and the triceps contracts.
3. The biceps and triceps of the upper arm work as a pair. When one contracts, the other relaxes.

## Think and Explore

1. How does the biceps feel when it contracts? When it relaxes?
2. How can you determine the strength of your arm?
3. Find two other pairs of opposing muscles working in your body.
4. Are there more muscles or bones in your body?

## Can You Build a Model Showing How an Arm Muscle Works?

### Materials

2 pieces of wood (about 2 inches x 10 inches)
hinge
long balloon
string

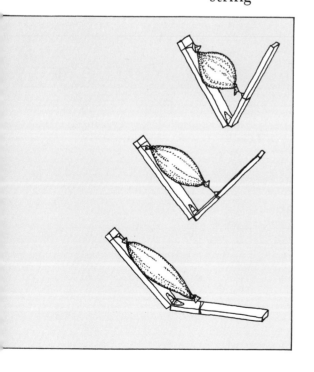

### Procedure

1. Join the 2 pieces of wood with a hinge as shown in the diagram. The wood represents the arm bones. The hinge represents the elbow joint.
2. Blow up the long balloon to about a quarter full.
3. Tie the two ends of the balloon to the wood pieces. The balloon represents the biceps muscle.
4. Open and close the wood pieces.
5. Record what you see.

## Conclusions

1. The closing and opening of the wood pieces causes the balloon to become shorter and puff out and to stretch long. This activity shows what happens to the biceps muscle when the arm closes and opens.
2. When the arm opens, the biceps muscle relaxes. When the arm closes, the biceps muscle contracts.

## Think and Explore

1. As seen from the arm model, what is one limitation of the elbow joint movement?
2. How could you build a different arm model with different materials?

## *How Can You Pull a Toe by the "String"?*

## Materials

chicken foot (obtain from a butcher)
knife
forceps

Note: If a chicken foot is not available, a chicken wing will produce similar results.

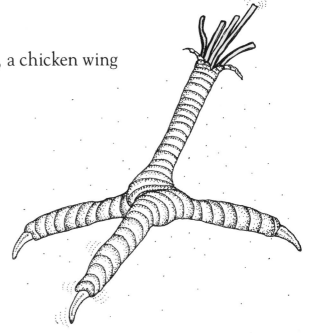

## Procedure

1. Trim the cut end of the chicken foot to expose the tendons. The tendons look like white cords.
2. Grasp the end of one tendon with a pair of forceps and pull.
3. Pull all the tendons, one at a time.
4. Record your observations.

## Conclusions

1. The tendons of the chicken foot are attached to the toe. When the tendons are pulled, the toe moves or curls.
2. You may find that there are several tendons attached to the same toe.

## Think and Explore

1. Suppose you cook a piece of meat with a lot of tendons in it. Would you expect the meat to be tender or chewy? Why?
2. Tom had a very bad accident. Several tendons of his wrist were cut. How may this accident affect his fingers? Explain why.

## How Do Cooking Methods Make Meat Tender or Tough?

**Do this activity under the supervision of an adult.**

## Materials

beef flank steak (obtain from your local supermarket)
magnifying glass
knife
frying pan
cooking oil
cooking spatula

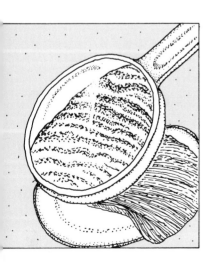

## Procedure

1. Examine a piece of flank steak carefully with a magnifying glass.
2. Cut the meat into two halves—A and B.

3. Cut meat A into 1/4-inch strips, cutting across the meat grain.
4. Cut meat B into 1/4-inch strips, cutting in the same direction as the meat grain.
5. Cook both A and B strips in a frying pan with a little cooking oil, keeping them separated.
6. Eat the meat after it is lightly cooked. Which strips are chewy? Which strips are tender?

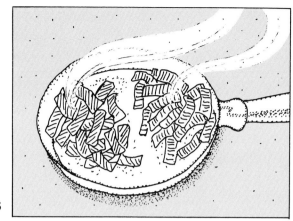

## Conclusions

1. Meat A is tender because the meat fibers have been broken into small pieces by cutting across the meat grain.
2. Meat B is chewy because the meat fibers are still in strips like strings as a result of cutting in the same direction as the meat grain.

## Think and Explore

1. When you prepare to cook meat, why is it important to find out the direction of the meat grain before the meat is cut?
2. You can slice a piece of meat very thin when it is semifrozen. Why do you think that is?
3. When you cook vegetables, such as celery, is it important to find out the directions of the plant fibers before they are cut? Why?

# *What Happens When Muscles Become Tired?*

## Materials
clock or watch with second hand

## Procedure

### Part A
1. Copy a paragraph from any page in this book.
2. Now move the fingers of your writing hand as if you were playing the piano. Move the fingers quickly. Keep moving them until they are tired.
3. Copy the same paragraph again.
4. Compare the writing in the two samples and record what you see.

### Part B
5. Raise one leg while seated on a chair. Record the time you started.
6. Keep your leg raised until it feels tired. Record the time when you put your leg down.
7. Figure how long you kept your leg raised.
8. Rest for 30 seconds and then repeat steps 5, 6, and 7.
9. Repeat step 8.
10. Compare the times recorded in steps 7, 8, and 9.

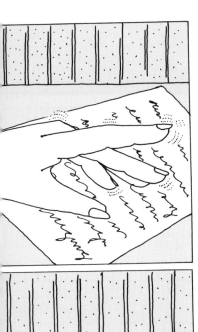

## Conclusions
1. Tired muscles affect how well you can do a task. You cannot write well when your finger muscles are tired.
2. Tired muscles affect how long you can do a task. You have to put your legs down when the leg

muscles are tired. As the muscles get more tired, the time you can spend doing a task will get shorter and shorter.

## Think and Explore

1. You want to improve your performance as a race cyclist. How would you plan to overcome the problem of tired muscles?
2. You can do ten push-ups. How would you go about increasing the number to fifty?

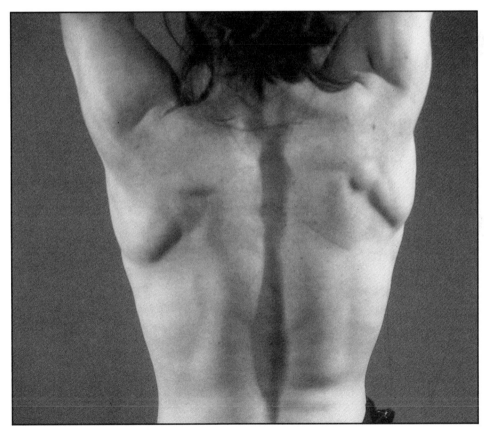

Back muscles

# Chapter 4

# The Circulatory System

**Key Terms**
- artery
- blood
- pulse
- vein

The circulatory system is a special kind of plumbing system. It has many pipes and a pump. The pipes are the blood vessels. The pump is the heart. The blood vessels carry a fluid called the blood. Blood brings needed supplies, such as dissolved food and oxygen, to all the cells of the body. In return, the blood removes wastes from the cells. This constant to-and-from movement of the blood is called circulation. Blood does other important jobs too. It keeps you warm, fights germs, and seals wounds in the skin.

When you were younger, you may have used a hollow rubber ball as a squirt gun. You punched a small hole in the ball and filled it with water. When you pumped the ball, the water shot out. Your heart works in somewhat the same way. It is hollow and is filled with blood. The heart is made of muscle and does its own pumping. Each time the heart muscle contracts, blood is forced out of the heart through blood vessels called the arteries. When the heart muscle relaxes, the heart opens up and blood flows in to fill it from blood vessels called veins. The heart as the pump is the center of the circulatory system. It is possible to check a part of the blood circulation by feeling the pulse. The pulse is the pumping force of the heart felt on the surface of a blood vessel. For example, you can feel the pulse on the surface of your inner wrist, just above the thumb. When the doctor examines you, he takes your pulse to find how well your heart is working.

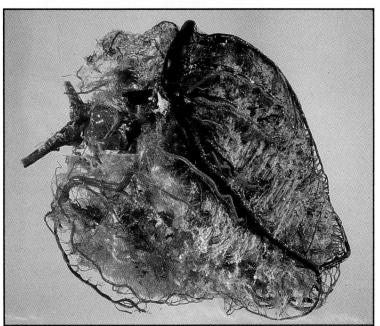

Cast of the inside of
a human heart

What is your definition of a healthy person? Some
people may use words that describe physical features,
such as *tall* and *muscular*. Actually physical features
are only a part of good health. Good health also
includes a strong, healthy heart. A healthy heart
allows you to do daily tasks and enjoy active leisure-
time pursuits. Such things as overeating, worrying,
and smoking can make the heart work harder, causing
heart trouble, such as a heart attack. Eating right and
exercising regularly for about 15 to 30 minutes a day
are suggested for maintaining a healthy heart.

## Facts
- The average person's body has about 60,000 miles
  (96,000 kilometers) of blood vessels.
- Your heart is about the size of your closed fist.
- The average person has about 9 to 10 pints (4.2 to
  4.7 liters) of blood.
- In one day the heart pumps about 2,000 gallons
  (75,706 liters) of blood through the body.
- Heart disease is the leading cause of death in the
  United States.
- The composition of blood is closest to seawater.

## How Can You Hear Your Own Heart?

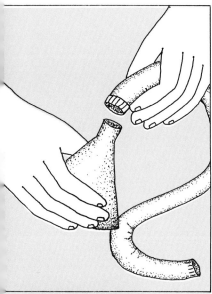

### Materials
small funnel
rubber tubing about 15 inches (38 centimeters)

### Procedure
1. Put the piece of rubber tubing over the small opening of the funnel.
2. Place the wide end of the funnel over your chest, positioning it approximately above the heart.
3. Hold the end of the rubber tubing against your ear.
4. Record what you hear.

### Conclusion
The heart sounds are heard as a long, loud "lubb" followed by a short, soft "dub." The "lubb" is called the first heart sound. The heart relaxes after the first sound. The "dub" is called the second heart sound. The heart contracts after the second heart sound. The sounds are caused by the sudden opening and closing of the heart valves.

### Think and Explore
1. How do you think the funnel works to help you hear your heartbeat?
2. How does the rubber tubing help you hear?
3. Count the number of your heartbeats in one minute. Remember, each beat has two sounds— "lubb-dub."

# *What Makes Your Heart Work Harder?*

## Materials
clock or watch with a second hand
paper
pencil

## Procedure
1.  Locate the big artery in your wrist just above the thumb. This is called the radial artery.
2.  Put your middle and index fingers on the wrist over the radial artery. Press gently until you feel the pulse beating.
3.  Count the pulse for a minute while you are sitting down quietly.
4.  Wait one minute and take your pulse again.
5.  Wait a minute and take your pulse a third time.
6.  Add the three counts and divide by three to get an average pulse count.
7.  Now take the pulse three times over a five-minute period while standing quietly. Average the three pulse counts.
8.  Run in place for about one minute. Take the pulse immediately after exercising.
9.  Compare the sitting, standing, and running pulses. Record with paper and pencil.

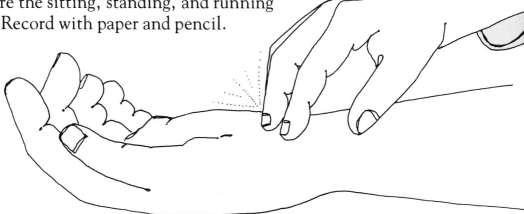

## Conclusion

The running pulse is the fastest, the standing pulse is in the middle, and the sitting pulse is the slowest. The pulse goes faster as you work harder—for example, standing straight and running—because the heart pumps faster to supply air and food to the body.

## Think and Explore

1. Predict what you think would happen to your pulse if you put one hand in a container of ice water. Why? Try it for a minute, then take your pulse.
2. What do you think very warm (but not boiling) water would do to your pulse? Why? Try it for a minute. Then count your pulse.

## *Can You See Your Pulse?*

## Materials

flat toothpick
thumbtack

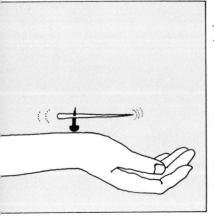

## Procedure

1. Put the sharp point of the thumbtack through the wide end of the toothpick. What you have made is called a pulsemeter.
2. Locate the radial pulse on your wrist. The pulse can be located at the wrist right above the thumb.
3. Place the pulsemeter on the pulse location.
4. Watch the pulsemeter carefully and record what you see happening.

## Conclusion
The toothpick vibrates with the beats of the pulse.

## Think and Explore
1. You can feel your pulse and you can also see your pulse. Which method is more accurate for recording your pulse?
2. Repeat the activity "What Makes Your Heart Work Harder?" with the pulsemeter and compare the results you get.

# How Hard Does the Heart Work?

## Materials
tennis ball
watch or clock with a second hand

## Procedure
1. Give the tennis ball a good hard squeeze. This is approximately the force that is required for your heart to pump in one beat.
2. Try to squeeze and release the tennis ball 70 times a minute. Record how your hand feels.

## Conclusion
Your hand and fingers will feel very tired after a minute of squeezing and releasing. You can try this for more than one minute if you are not convinced. What happens to the force and speed of your squeezing?

## Think and Explore

1. Why does the heart need to pump the blood to the lungs and back to the heart?
2. Which of the following is the strongest muscle of the group: the upper arm muscle, the heart muscle, or the thigh muscle? Explain your answer.

## How Does the Circulatory System Work?

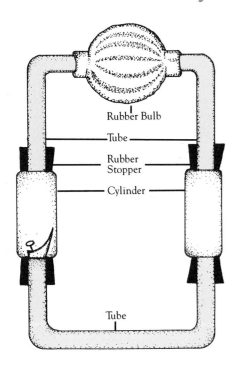

### Materials

rubber bulb with 2 openings
plastic sheet
pin
transparent rubber tubing
4 rubber stoppers
2 transparent cylinders with 2 openings
red dye

### Procedure

1. Set up a model of the circulatory system as shown in the diagram.
2. Squeeze and release the bulb continuously until you see something happen.
3. Record your observations.

## Conclusions

1. The red fluid inside the tube flows in one direction in a circular pattern.
2. The plastic sheet held by the pin opens and closes.

## Think and Explore

1. What makes the red fluid (which represents the blood) flow in one direction?
2. What is the function of the plastic sheet that is held by the pin?
3. What is the function of the rubber bulb?
4. The model simulates the actions of two kinds of blood vessels: veins and arteries. Try to identify the kinds of blood vessels represented in the circulation model (hint: examine the direction of flow of each tube section of the model).

## *How Does Blood Flow in Blood Vessels?*

**Do this activity under the supervision of an adult.**

## Materials

goldfish
1-gallon fish tank with water
ether
small fishnet
petri dish
cotton
2 microscope glass slides
microscope

## Procedure

1. Put the goldfish in the 1-gallon tank. Add 2 to 3 drops of ether to knock out the fish. *Caution: Ether is dangerous. It is poisonous. Don't inhale the vapor; it is harmful.*

2. When the fish rolls on its side, remove it with a small fishnet. Put the fish in a petri dish.
3. Cover the fish's body with water-soaked cotton and expose the tail. Place the tail carefully between the two glass slides.
4. Keep the cotton wet with water. This will keep the fish alive.
5. Put the fish under the microscope. Look for blood flow near the edge of the tail. If blood stops flowing in the blood vessels, put the fish back in the tank without the ether.
6. Observe what you see with the microscope and draw some sketches.

## Conclusions

1. Depending on the power of the microscope, you should be able to see small blood vessels near the edge of the tail.
2. Blood cells are seen as small discs inside the blood vessels.
3. Blood flows most of the time continuously in the same direction.

## Think and Explore

1. How wide is a small blood vessel as compared with the blood cells?
2. Press your finger into your hand. Watch the skin turn pale and then red again. Explain why this happens.
3. How are small blood vessels helpful in the fish's tail? In your body?

# Chapter 5

# The Breathing System

Since birth you have been breathing in and out between ten and fifteen times every minute without having to think about it. Let us follow some air into your body and explore the parts of the breathing system. The air enters the nose or mouth and moves down into the windpipe. Run your fingers up and down your throat. The little rings you feel are the cartilage of the windpipe. The cartilage rings keep the windpipe firm and open. Air moves down the windpipe into the lungs. In the lungs the windpipe divides into small branches that finally lead into air sacs. All the air sacs are surrounded by blood vessels. It is at this air sac-blood vessel junction that air exchanges. Oxygen moves from the lungs to supply the blood vessels. Carbon dioxide and water move as wastes from the blood vessels into the lungs. Essentially, the breathing system (the nose, windpipe, and lungs) lets oxygen into the body and removes carbon dioxide and water vapor.

Why is the exchange of air so important to our bodies? A cell in the body may be compared with a flame. Just as a flame must have oxygen to keep burning, so must a cell have oxygen to stay alive. Did you know that a person can stay alive without food for weeks and without water for days but without air for only a few minutes? More importantly, the cells must be supplied with oxygen to release the energy locked up in the food materials. And we know that energy is vital to many important life activities. In short, you must breathe to stay alive.

**Key Terms**
- carbon dioxide
- control
- diaphragm
- indicator
- mucus
- oxygen
- phenolphthalein

Coughing, sneezing, hiccupping, crying, and laughing are all different forms of breathing. These breathing reactions are caused in various ways. For example, dust in the air can irritate the nose and bring on sneezing. Dust particles in the windpipe or excess mucus can cause coughing. Eating certain foods can bring on sharp contractions of the diaphragm muscles, resulting in hiccups. Crying and laughing are special breathing reactions to emotions.

The air we breathe also plays an important part in speaking. The voice box at the top of the windpipe is responsible for making sound. It contains the vocal cords, which vibrate to produce a series of different notes. However, these notes are modified to the different sounds of our speech by the use of the teeth, tongue, lips, mouth, and nose.

The efficiency of the lungs to supply oxygen to the body is sometimes used as a measure of physical fitness. If you are soon out of breath when you do some active work, then maybe your breathing system is not in good shape. To shape up your breathing system, you need to increase the amount of air your lungs can hold (lung volume). A large lung volume means that you can take in more oxygen when your body needs it. For example, you would expect the lung volume of an Olympic runner to be greater than that of an office worker. And if that office worker runs every morning, he or she would have a greater lung volume than one who doesn't exercise. Regular exercise is effective in increasing lung volume and developing a healthy breathing system.

Serious disorders of the breathing system lead to early death. Cigarette smoking is related to many types of diseases and disorders, including cancer of

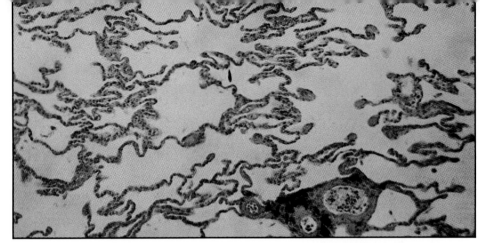

Microscopic slide of a normal lung

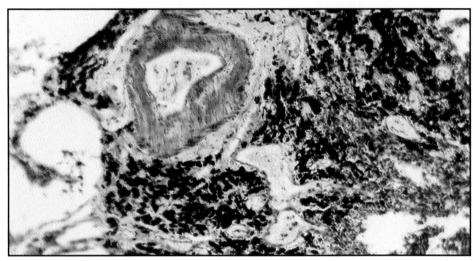

Microscopic slide of a diseased lung with carbon deposits. Sometimes this condition is called "black lung."

the lungs, lips, and voice box. The best advice on cigarette smoking is still that given by the American Heart Association: BE SMART—DON'T START.

## Facts
- The lungs are made of about 5 hundred million (500,000,000) air sacs.
- Breathing is controlled by the brain. However, we can override the control briefly by either holding our breath or panting.
- The amount of carbon dioxide gas in the blood is important in regulating breathing.
- A loud voice requires a big gush of air passing across the vocal cords.

# How Do the Lungs Work?

## Materials
bicycle pump
fresh beef lungs with windpipe intact (obtain from the
butcher shop)
rubber tubing

## Procedure
1. Attach the bicycle pump to the windpipe of the
beef lungs. You may connect the rubber tubing
between the pump and the windpipe of the lungs.
2. Start pumping the bicycle pump. Record your
observation.

## Conclusion
As the piston of the pump is pushed, air rushes into
the air sacs causing the lungs to inflate.

## Think and Explore
1. Why is it important that the beef lungs be fresh for
this activity?
2. Lift the lungs in your hand. Are they light or
heavy? Why?
3. Cut off a piece of the beef lung and put it in water.
What happens? How do you explain this?
4. Touch the windpipe. How does it feel in
comparison with the lungs? Explain the difference.
5. In what way is the activity like human breathing?

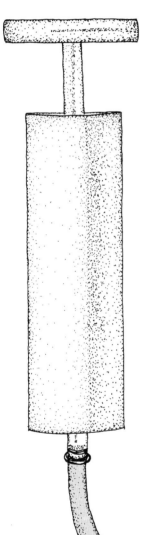

## Can You Simulate Breathing by Building a Model?

### Materials
bell jar
Y-shaped glass tube
3 balloons
string
rubber stopper
Vaseline (for sliding tube through stopper)

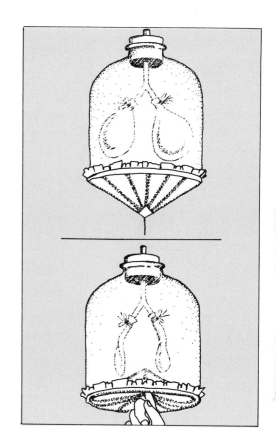

### Procedure
1. Build a glass lung model following the diagram shown.
2. To make the model breathe in, pull the diaphragm down. Record your observation.
3. To make the model breathe out, return the diaphragm to its original level position. Record your observations.

### Conclusions
1. The balloons inflate when the diaphragm is in the down position.
2. The balloons deflate when the diaphragm is in the level position.

### Think and Explore
1. What parts of the human breathing system do the balloons, the Y-shaped tube, and the glass bell jar represent?

2. Put your hands under your ribs and feel the diaphragm muscle. Which part of the model represents the diaphragm?
3. With the help of the model, find out how your diaphragm helps you to breathe.
4. What happens to the breathing system when the glass bell jar is not airtight?
5. How would a hole in the chest make breathing very difficult and why might it lead to death?

## How Much Air Do Your Lungs Hold in One Breath?

### Materials
gallon jar
grease pen
water
cardboard
dishpan
rubber tube

### Procedure
1. Mark the jar in quarters with a grease pen, starting at the bottom—1/4, 1/2, and 3/4.
2. Fill the jar with water. Make sure that the jar is so full that the water almost spills off the top.
3. Cover the mouth of the jar with a piece of cardboard.
4. Holding the cardboard in place, place the mouth of the jar in a dishpan containing water.
5. Slowly slide the cardboard off the mouth of the jar under water.
6. Slip the rubber tube into the jar. Leave one end of the tube out of the water.

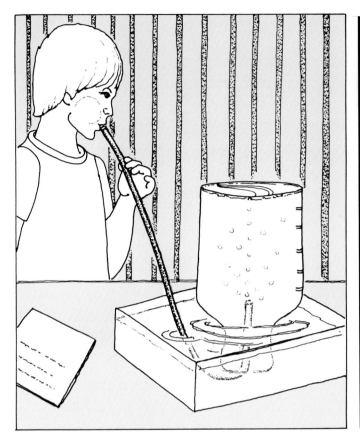

7. Take a deep breath and blow into the tube.
8. Record what happens and the new water level inside the jar.

## Conclusions
1. Water in the jar is forced out and replaced by the air blown into the tube.
2. The new water level inside the jar represents the volume of air the lungs hold in one breath.

## Think and Explore
1. Is the volume of air held in one breath the same as the total lung volume? Why?
2. Is the lung volume related to any of these: weight, height, age, sex? Support your answer.
3. What do you suggest to improve the accuracy of the experiment?

## *What Is in Breath?*

### Materials
mirror
drinking straw
limewater (calcium hydroxide solution)

### Procedure
1. Breathe onto the mirror and record your observation.
2. Blow gently through the straw into a glass of limewater. What do you observe?

### Conclusions
1. A film of water vapor is formed on the mirror. Your breath contains water vapor. The vapor condenses on the cool surface of the mirror.
2. The limewater is turned cloudy by your breath. The cloudiness is caused by the formation of a fine white solid called calcium carbonate. The chemical reaction shows that your breath contains carbon dioxide.

### Think and Explore
1. Where do the water vapor and carbon dioxide of your breath come from?
2. Why does your body have to get rid of water vapor and carbon dioxide?

# How Much Carbon Dioxide Do You Produce in Your Breath?

## Materials

measuring cup or cylinder
2 bottles
eyedropper
phenolphthalein (an indicator obtained from a
   chemical supply store)
sodium hydroxide solution
drinking straw

## Procedure

1. Measure 100 milliliters (about 3 ounces) of water into a bottle.

2. Add 5 drops of phenolphthalein and stir. Phenolphthalein is an indicator. In the presence of an acid, such as lemon juice or vinegar, the indicator is colorless; in the presence of a base, such as soap solution or caustic soda, it is red. If the water remains colorless, that means that there is carbon dioxide in the water, since carbon dioxide and water together produce a mild acid called carbonic acid.

3. To get rid of the carbon dioxide, add sodium hydroxide solution slowly, drop by drop, stirring after each drop. Continue until the solution turns pink in color. The

sodium hydroxide solution neutralizes the carbon dioxide. How many drops of sodium hydroxide did you add? Keep this bottle, called a control, for color comparison.

4. Measure about 100 milliliters of water into another bottle. Add 5 drops of phenolphthalein and stir.

5. Sit quietly for one minute. Then bubble your breath into the second bottle for one minute.

6. Add sodium hydroxide solution drop by drop, stirring after each drop. Continue until the same pink color is obtained as in the control bottle. The procedure described is called a carbon dioxide test. How many drops did you add?

7. Copy the following table. Record the number of drops it took to neutralize the carbon dioxide in the control bottle and the carbon dioxide you breathed into the test bottle while you were sitting still.

## Measuring Carbon Dioxide In Your Breath

| Procedure | Drops of Sodium Hydroxide |
|---|---|
| control bottle | _____ |
| sitting quietly | _____ |
| walking | _____ |
| running | _____ |

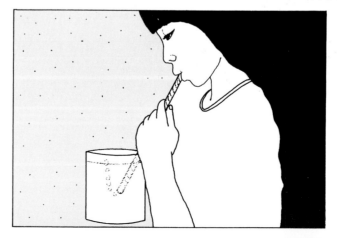

8. Wash the test bottle thoroughly. Refill with water and phenolphthalein as in step 4.
9. Exercise mildly by walking around for one minute.
10. Repeat the carbon dioxide test. Record the number of drops of sodium hydroxide used.
11. Wash and refill the bottle again.
12. Exercise by running in place for one minute. Repeat the carbon dioxide test and record your result in the table.

## Conclusion

It takes more drops of sodium hydroxide solution to neutralize the carbon dioxide after the running exercise. This shows that running produces more carbon dioxide than walking or sitting still.

## Think and Explore

1. Why does running produce more carbon dioxide than walking and sitting?
2. Which of the following requires more oxygen: running, walking, or sitting? How do you support your answer?
3. As you use more energy, what happens to the rate of breathing? Why?
4. What was the purpose of setting up a control bottle in the experiment? Can the experiment work accurately without the control? Explain.
5. As the body produces more carbon dioxide, as in running, the system will become more acid. How does your body system adjust to this extra acid?

## *Is Cigarette Smoking Really Harmful?*

> **Do this activity under the supervision of an adult.**

### Materials
glass bottle
water
2-hole rubber stopper
glass tubing
pinch clamp
2 cigarettes (one with a filter tip and the other without)

rubber tube
stand with a holder
beaker
matches

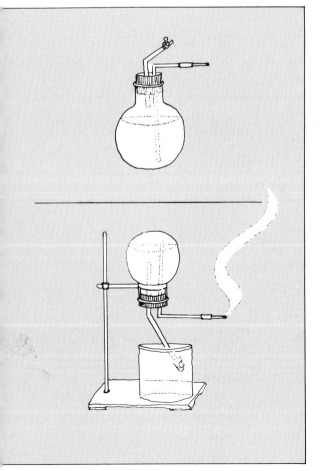

### Procedure
1. Set up the apparatus as shown.
2. Turn the apparatus upside down.
3. Light the cigarette. Continue the smoking process by opening the pinch clamp very slowly. The water drained from the bottle will create a suction force to keep the cigarette smoking.
4. Allow the cigarette to burn. Record your observations.
5. Repeat the experiment with the second cigarette. Record your observations.
6. Pour out the water after the experiment has been completed. Notice how it smells. Examine the inner surface of the bottle. What do you see?

## Conclusions

1. The color of the water in the bottle looks blackish and dirty. This dirt is caused by tars from the smoked cigarette.
2. The color of the water in the bottle looks a little cleaner with the filter tip cigarette, as some of the impurities are trapped by the filter tip.
3. The dirty water in the bottle smells bad.

## Think and Explore

1. Where do the tars in cigarettes come from?
2. Where in your body might tars collect after you have been smoking?
3. What conclusion do you draw about the ability of the filter tip to remove all tars?
4. How can you be a passive smoker when you go into a room where people are smoking?
5. A smoker coughs more often than a nonsmoker. Why do you think this happens?
6. Every pack of cigarettes has a side label that contains a warning from the surgeon general of the United States. One such warning says, "SURGEON GENERAL'S WARNING: Smoking Causes Lung Cancer, Heart Disease, Emphysema, And May Complicate Pregnancy." In your opinion, how accurate is this statement?
7. How can you convince a friend that he or she should not start smoking?
8. What changes could you make so that the experiment would show other bad effects of cigarette smoking?

## Chapter 6

# The Digestive System

The human body is a machine that is built and fueled by food. Like the food you eat, your body is made of water, protein, fat, carbohydrates, and salts. The statement "You are what you eat" makes sense, then, doesn't it?

What about the foods you choose to fuel your body? Will eating carrots sharpen your eyesight? Does eating fish make you a smarter person? In order to answer such questions, you need to know something about foods and the body's food requirements. To stay in good health, a person needs to eat a balanced diet. This diet supplies the right kinds and amounts of food to give nourishment and energy for body uses. In a balanced diet, there are four important groups of food: (1) the bread-cereal group, (2) milk foods, (3) meat and fish, and (4) vegetables and fruits.

Weight control is an important part of your health. In this country, only one out of five overweight persons reaches the age of seventy. Heart disease and other illnesses are common problems among overweight people. A healthy person should avoid taking in more calories (a measurement of the energy in different foods) than the body can use. In other words, do not overeat, and choose a balanced diet.

How does the body put this food to good use? You will have a better understanding of the digestive system if you think of it as a donut. The digestive tract (the hole of the donut), though inside the body, is still outside the body cells (the donut). Clearly, if food is to be used, it must cross the walls of the digestive tract into the body cells. The main purpose of digestion is to break down food so that its nutrients can be taken into the body cells.

Digestion is a long step-by-step process that is carried on in the mouth, the stomach, the small intestine, and the large intestine. The breakdown of food first takes place in the mouth. The teeth chop and grind the food. Saliva from the salivary glands prepares starchy food for digestion. The material is then swallowed and pushed through a tube called the esophagus to a pouch called the stomach. In the stomach all food is stored temporarily. Any protein in that food is partially digested. The next stop is the small intestine, where chemicals from the liver and pancreas feed in. The digestion of starch, protein, and fats is completed in the small intestine. The digested food still cannot serve the body until it gets into the cells. In the small intestine, the digested food becomes so small that it can pass through the wall of the intestine. This process is called absorption. The absorbed food is then carried by the blood vessels to all the body cells. The last step in digestion takes place in the large intestine, where water is absorbed from any undigested material and waste is disposed of.

## Facts
- In 1822 Dr. William Beaumont drew some juice from the stomach of a patient. He put the juice into a bottle and dropped a piece of meat into it. The meat was digested and gone in about ten hours!
- Your digestive tract is about 30.35 feet (9.25 meters) long.

- In the course of digestion, food remains in the stomach for as long as six hours.
- Many doctors now believe that plant fibers in the diet can help prevent the development of cancer of the digestive tract.
- Carbohydrates, fats, and proteins are good sources of energy. Fats, in particular, can give us the most energy. Fifteen milliliters (1/2 ounce) of fat yields about 100 calories.
- A normal active boy of fifteen needs an average of 3,000 calories per day. In contrast, an average active girl of fifteen needs only 2,500 calories per day.
- A 100-pound (45.4 kilograms) person uses 50 calories per hour for sleeping and 200 calories per hour for active play.

Drawing of the human digestive system

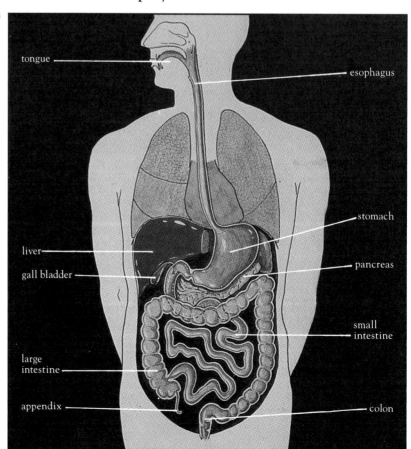

## How Does Food Move Through the Digestive Tract?

### Materials
marbles
rubber tube (diameter slightly smaller than the
    marbles)

### Procedure
1. Wet the inside of the rubber tube. The tube
   represents the food tube called the digestive tract.
2. Put several marbles into the tube. The marbles
   represent food inside the digestive tract.
3. Squeeze the tube with your hand in a forward
   direction. The movement is like the muscular
   squeeze, called peristalsis, of the digestive tract.
4. Record your observations.

### Conclusion
The marbles are squeezed from one end of the tube
(the digestive tract) to the other.

### Think and Explore
1. Where does peristalsis start and end in the
   digestive tract?
2. Is this statement always true: Peristalsis works in
   one direction? Explain?
3. How can you control the movement of food
   materials through the digestive tract? Explain.
4. What prevents food materials from moving straight
   through the digestive tract?
5. Does digestion take place before, after, or during
   peristalsis? Why?

# How Does Saliva Work?

## Materials
soda crackers
bread

## Procedure
1. Put a few pieces of a soda cracker in your mouth.
2. Chew the cracker for 1 minute before swallowing.
3. Describe the taste (a) when you started chewing and (b) after 1 minute.
4. Rinse your mouth with water and repeat steps 1, 2, and 3 with a piece of bread.

## Conclusion
The cracker/bread tastes bland when you start chewing. After a minute the cracker/bread tastes a little sweet. This change of taste indicates the chemical change of starchy food (with the bland taste) to simple sugar (with the sweet taste) by the action of the saliva.

## Think and Explore
1. Is the saliva in your mouth sweet? How can you find out?
2. How does saliva change the cracker/bread besides changing the taste?
3. How do your teeth take part in the digestion of the food you eat?

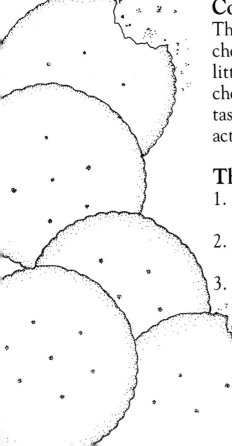

# How Can You Identify Nutrients in a Food?

This activity has four parts. Each part is a test for a different nutrient.

## A. Testing for Simple Sugar

### Materials
Benedict's solution
milk
test tube
test-tube holder
alcohol burner

### Procedure
1. Pour equal amounts of milk and Benedict's solution into the test tube.
2. Using the test-tube holder, heat the test tube gently over an alcohol burner by moving the tube back and forth over the flame. Point the mouth of the test tube away from yourself and anyone else.
3. Record your observations.

### Conclusion
The color of the solution changes from green to yellow and finally to red. The color change of the Benedict's solution shows that there is sugar in milk.

### Think and Explore

1. How long will the color of the Benedict's solution remain red? Can the color change back to green? How can you find out?
2. How can you use the Benedict's solution to test for simple sugars in an apple? In tap water?

## B.  Testing for Protein

### Materials
egg
biuret solution
test tube

### Procedure

1. Crack open the egg and separate the white from the yolk.
2. Put the egg white in a test tube.
3. Pour a little biuret solution into the test tube.
4. Record your observations.

### Conclusion

The solution turns purple. The change of color indicates that there is protein in the egg white.

### Think and Explore

1. What will happen to the biuret solution if you test the egg yolk?
2. What other foods will turn the biuret solution purple? How can you experiment?

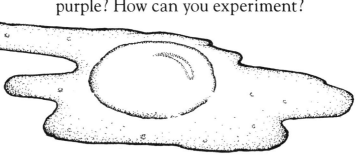

## C. Testing for Starch

### Materials
potato
iodine solution
eyedropper

### Procedure
1. Slice off a piece of the potato.
2. Place a few drops of iodine solution on the slice.
3. Record your observations.

### Conclusion
Dark blue or blue-black stains appear on the potato. This change of color shows that there is starch in foods. Starch is a form of stored sugar in potato.

### Think and Explore
What do you think would be the result of the starch test on foods such as onion slices, apple slices, and lemon slices?

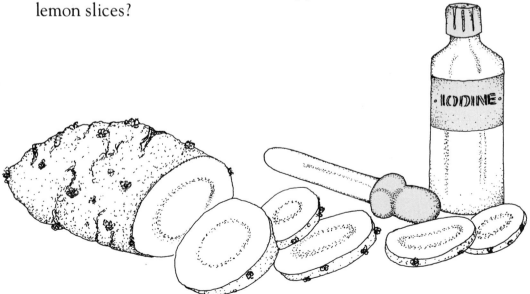

# D. Testing for Fat

## Materials
2 pieces of brown paper
peanut butter

## Procedure
1. Spread some peanut butter on one piece of brown paper.
2. Place the second piece of brown paper on the peanut butter. Rub the two pieces of brown paper together.
3. Hold the paper against a light source and record your observations.

## Conclusion
Grease spots appear on the brown paper. These spots are translucent against a light source. The grease spots in the test show that there are fats in the food.

## Think and Explore
1. Can the grease spot on a piece of brown paper tell you how much fat is in a food? Explain.
2. Which of the following contains fat: a peanut, lettuce, milk, an egg, or bread?

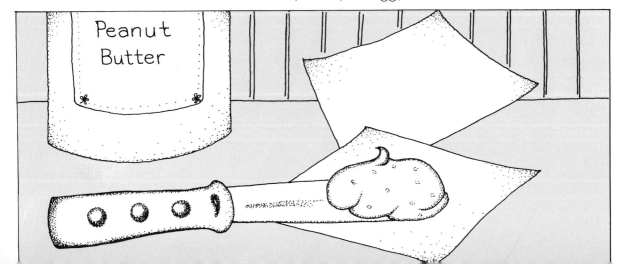

3. Do you agree or disagree with the following statements? Explain.
   a. Tomato or citrus juice helps digestion.
   b. Milk helps build stronger teeth.
   c. Butter has more calories than margarine.
   d. A person can lose weight by eating less.
   e. As much as possible, food should be eaten raw.
   f. Some foods cannot be eaten together; for example, honey and bean curd.
   g. Junk food has zero nutrition value.
   h. Vitamin C can help to cure the common cold.
4. Based on your knowledge of the different nutrient tests and foods, complete the following table. The first example is already done for you.
   **Hints:**
   a. Fruits and vegetables have plenty of carbohydrates, some starch, and no fat.
   b. Meat is rich in protein. The amount of fat in meat varies.
   c. Dairy products contain mostly protein and fat.
   d. Cereals are rich in carbohydrates. Some also contain protein.

## The Nutrients Identification Table

| Foods | Fats | Starch | Protein |
|---|---|---|---|
| bread | no | yes | yes |
| potato | | | |
| orange | | | |
| meat | | | |
| apple | | | |
| noodle | | | |
| cheese | | | |
| Jell-O | | | |
| carrot | | | |
| fish | | | |

## How Many Food Calories Do You Need Each Day?

### Materials
food labels or a calorie chart (some cookbooks contain
  such charts)

### Procedure
1. Collect as many food labels as you can from
   canned or prepared foods. These labels give the
   number of calories in average-size servings of food.
   If you don't have labels, use the calorie chart.
2. List each food that you eat for one day.
3. Use the food labels or the calorie chart to count
   the number of calories in the foods you listed. Total
   the calories. How many did you take in at each
   meal? For the whole day?
4. Compare your calorie count with the requirements
   shown in the following table.

| Calorie Requirement Table | | | | | | | |
|---|---|---|---|---|---|---|---|
| **Age** | 10 | 11 | 12 | 13 | 14 | 15 | 16 |
| **Girls** | 2,200 | 2,250 | 2,300 | 2,350 | 2,400 | 2,450 | 2,475 (calories) |
| **Boys** | 2,400 | 2,450 | 2,500 | 2,750 | 3,000 | 3,200 | 3,300 (calories) |

### Conclusion
Your calorie count may differ from the table,
depending upon what you eat every day.

## Think and Explore

1. If your calorie count is less than what is recommended by the table, how do you plan to increase your calorie intake?
2. If your calorie count is more than what is recommended by the table, how do you plan to decrease your calorie intake?
3. What foods give you the most calories according to the food labels or calorie chart?
4. In your opinion how accurate is the following statement: Your weight at the ages of twenty-five and fifty-five should be about the same.
5. What are some of the common causes for people becoming overweight?

## Is Milk Really the Perfect Food?

### Materials

| | |
|---|---|
| heavy cream | vinegar |
| test tube | filter funnel |
| lactic acid | filter paper |
| shallow pan | beaker |
| hot plate | pot |

### Procedure

1. Pour some cream into the test tube. Then add a few drops of lactic acid.
2. Shake the tube vigorously until butter is formed on the top.

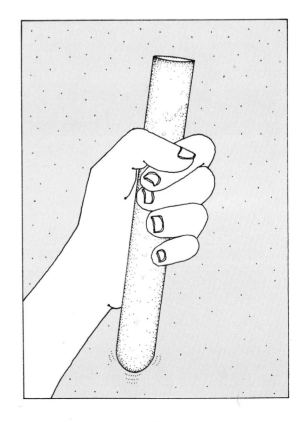

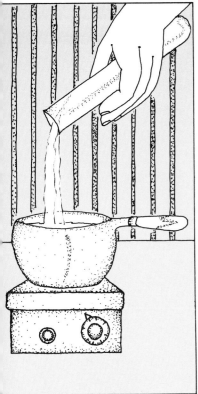

3. Skim off the butter and pour the liquid into a pan. Heat the liquid over a hot plate.
4. Add a few drops of vinegar to the liquid. The liquid will curdle.
5. Pour the curdled liquid through a filter with filter paper in it. Record what you see on the filter paper.
6. Boil the filtrate (the liquid that goes through the filter) and filter the liquid again using new filter paper. Record what remains on the filter paper.
7. Boil away the remaining liquid in a steam bath (a pot of water over a hot plate). What is left?

## Conclusions

1. Butter is formed in step 2.
2. The curd on the filter paper in step 5 is used to make cheese.
3. What is left on the filter paper in step 6 is albumin, a rich protein.
4. What is left on the filter paper in step 7 is milk sugar.

## Think and Explore

1. Identify all the nutrients that you have extracted from the milk.
2. Use the nutrient tests from "How Can You Identify Nutrients in a Food?" to confirm your identification.
3. Four glasses of milk a day are recommended for teenagers and pregnant women. How would you explain why teenagers and pregnant women need the same amount of milk each day?

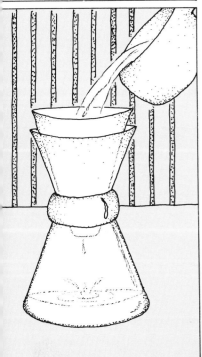

## How Does Digested Food Get Into the Body?

### Materials
sugar solution
red dye
artificial intestine (sausage casing obtained from a
   sausage shop)
string
jar

### Procedure
1. Prepare a sugar solution by mixing
   1 teaspoon of sugar to 1 cup of
   warm water.
2. Add a few drops of red dye to the
   sugar solution.
3. Tie one end of the intestine with
   a string. Fill the intestine 3/4 full
   with the red sugar solution. Close
   the other end of the intestine by
   tying it with a string.
4. Put the prepared intestine in a
   jar of water.
5. Wait a few hours and record your
   observation.

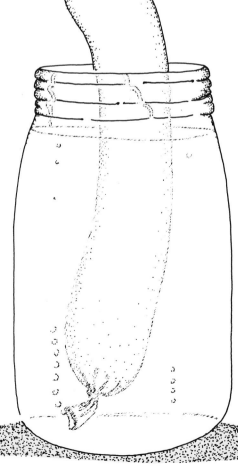

## Conclusion

Water from the jar moves through the skin of the intestine, causing the intestine to inflate. The water, representing digested food, is able to move across the intestinal wall by a process called absorption.

## Think and Explore

1. Why does the intestine allow water from the jar to be absorbed?
2. What would happen if plain water were put inside the intestine? Would the water in the jar be absorbed? How do you explain this?
3. Inside your intestine, which food materials can be absorbed and which cannot be absorbed?
4. What good is digestion if there is no absorption?
5. An overweight person reduced his weight by the surgical removal of a section of his small intestine. Why did he lose weight?

# Chapter 7

# The Waste-Disposal System

It is impossible to keep a place clean if you do not have a wastebasket or some other way of getting rid of wastes. Do you remember the last time the garbage collectors in your city were on strike? The environment must have been dirty and smelly. Similarly, if wastes are not removed from the body, the body environment will get dirty and, worse yet, sickness and death may also result. For this reason, the waste-disposal system is important to the body.

The human body produces several kinds of waste. These wastes include sweat, carbon dioxide gas, feces, and urine. The body removes the wastes in different ways. Water vapor and carbon dioxide are exhaled by the lungs. Undigested materials are passed out by the large intestine as feces. Other chemicals, especially those of the nitrogen group, are disposed of through the kidneys as urine and to some extent through the skin as sweat.

Your body has two bean-shaped kidneys. These lie just inside the back body wall under the last two pairs of ribs. The kidneys have two important jobs. The first is to keep the materials that the body needs. These materials can be water, sugar, and protein. The second is to get rid of wastes. The two jobs are carried out by a process called filtration. Filtration in the kidneys separates nonwaste and waste materials in the blood. Nonwaste materials are taken back by the body through the circulatory system. Wastes from the kidneys are carried out in a fluid called urine. The urine flows to the bladder for short-time storage.

**Key Terms**
- Benedict's solution
- bladder
- diabetes
- diabetic
- feces
- filtration
- glucose
- urine

When the bladder fills, the urine is passed to the outside of the body voluntarily. Because babies do not yet have bladder control, they wet themselves. Bladder control develops with time.

When you go for a checkup, your doctor may ask you for a urine sample. Do you know why? The answer is that the doctor can tell the condition of your kidneys by examining the urine. For example, blood in the urine may mean that there is bleeding in the kidneys. Glucose (a sugar) in the urine may indicate a hormonal defect called diabetes. A person with diabetes cannot retain blood glucose, and the glucose is passed out in the urine. Other kidney diseases are caused by very small agents called bacteria. Unhygienic personal habits increase the chance of kidney infection.

Sometimes the kidneys do not work properly and a man-made kidney has to be used. This man-made kidney is actually a filter machine. It works by

Healthy kidney

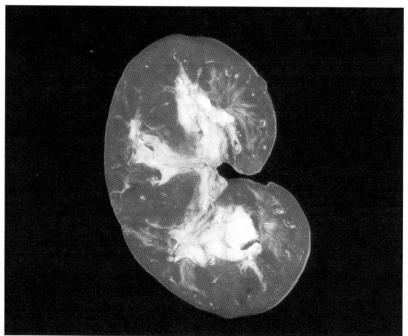

pumping blood through the machine. Waste materials are separated and clean filtered blood is then returned to the body.

## Facts

- A normal human kidney is about 5 inches (12 centimeters) long, 3 inches (7 centimeters) wide, and 1 inch (3 centimeters) thick.
- In 24 hours about 180 quarts (170 liters) of fluids are filtered through the kidneys.
- Of all the fluid filtered by the kidneys, only 1 percent is discarded as urine.
- The action of the kidneys is controlled by the brain.
- The bladder of an adult can hold about 1/3 quart (350 milliliters) of urine.
- Normal urine is made up of water, salts, and waste materials.
- Sweat and urine are liquid wastes that have similar compositions.

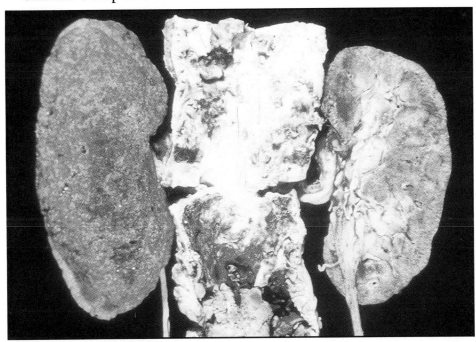

Diseased kidneys

## How Does Sweating Keep You Cool?

| **Do this activity under the supervision of an adult.** |
| --- |

## Materials
kettle
water
2 tall glasses
2 cloth strips
4 thermometers
electric pan

## Procedure
1. Heat the water in the kettle to about 104° F (40° C).
2. Fill the two glasses with the same amount of heated water.
3. Wet one cloth strip with the heated water. Wrap the wet strip in layers around the glass.
4. Wrap the other glass with the dry cloth, layering the cloth.
5. Place one thermometer in each glass.
6. Place another thermometer just under the top layer of the cloth strip wrapped around each glass.
7. Place the two glasses on a table.
8. Turn on the electric fan and direct the breeze of the fan toward the two glasses.
9. Observe and record the temperature of the four thermometers at one-minute intervals for fifteen minutes.
10. Plot the temperature changes on a graph.

## Conclusions

1. The temperature of the water in the two glasses decreases over the fifteen minutes.
2. The temperature of the water in the glass with the wet cloth strip decreases more rapidly than the other. The glass with the wet cloth strip represents a warm body covered with sweat. A sweating body cools faster than a dry body.

## Think and Explore

1. Which of the jobs done by sweating is more important, keeping your body cool or getting rid of wastes? Explain.
2. What are some of the other ways that your body helps you cool off?
3. People can sweat, but dogs cannot. How does a dog keep itself cool?
4. What does sweat taste like? What do you think sweat is made of?
5. Is it possible to get warm without sweating? Explain your answer.
6. When you are very warm, your breath is hot. Why do you think this happens?

Droplets of perspiration on skin

## How Does Filtration Work in the Kidneys?

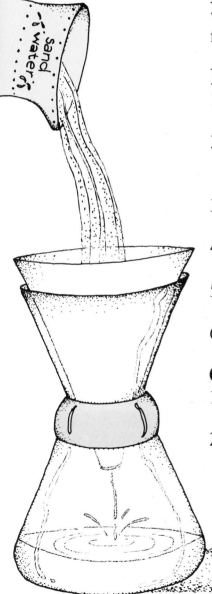

### Materials
round piece of filter paper
funnel
jar
water
fine sand

### Procedure
1. Fold the filter paper in half twice. Open it out to form a cone.
2. Place the cone with the pointed end first into the filter funnel. Wet the cone to make it stay in the funnel.
3. Position the filter funnel with the filter paper over a glass jar.
4. Mix a small pinch of fine sand with water. Stir well.
5. Pour the sand-water mixture slowly into the filter funnel.
6. Record your observations.

### Conclusions
1. The water slowly drips through the filter funnel into the jar below.
2. The fine sand is retained by the filter paper. Thus the water and the sand are separated by the filter paper. This process is called filtration.

## Think and Explore

1. What is the force that pushes the water through the filter paper?
2. What is the force that pushes the blood through the kidneys?
3. How are the filter paper and the kidneys similar?
4. A small trace of fine sand is found in the jar below the filter funnel. It is normal. Can you explain? Compare this situation with what happens when a kidney is diseased.
5. Examine the filtered water in the jar carefully. How does the examination show the condition (good or bad) of the filter paper? Can you see any similarity between the filtered water examination and a urine examination? What is one important way in which the filtered water is not like urine?

## *How Can You Test Urine for Glucose (A Sugar)?*

## Materials

urine sample
clean glass jar
Benedict's solution
alcohol burner
Clinitest pills (from a drugstore)
test tube
test-tube holder (clamp)

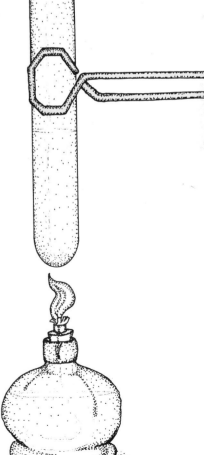

# A. The Benedict's Solution Test

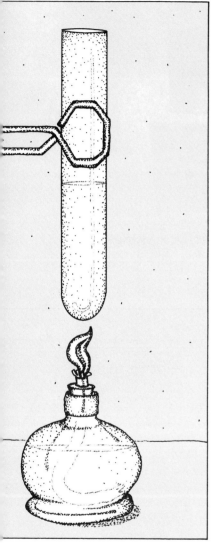

| **Do this activity under the supervision of an adult.** |

## Procedure

Do not eat any sweets for 24 hours before the test.
1. Obtain the urine sample first thing in the morning and save it in the clean glass jar.
2. Transfer a small amount of urine to a test tube.
3. Pour some Benedict's solution into the urine in the test tube.
4. Hold the test tube with a holder. Heat the tube over an alcohol burner. Make sure that you point the mouth of the tube away from yourself and other people.
5. Observe and record any color change.

## Conclusions

1. No change of color shows that the urine sample has no glucose. This test result indicates that the person has healthy kidneys, with no sign of diabetes.
2. An orange or red color indicates that the urine sample contains glucose. This test result shows that the person may be a diabetic (a person with diabetes) and should see a doctor for further testing.

# B. The Clinitest Pills

## Procedure

1. Put a small amount of the urine in a test tube.
2. Add a Clinitest pill to the test tube.
3. Record your observations.

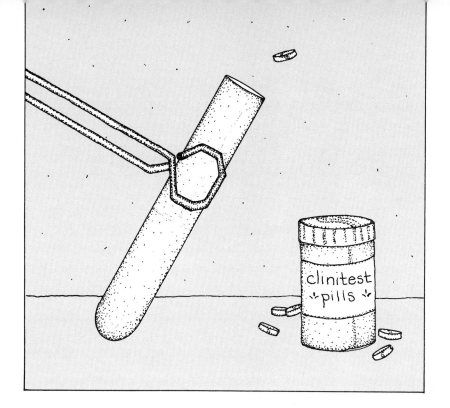

## Results

1. No change in color indicates that the urine contains no glucose. This test result shows that the person has healthy kidneys, with no diabetes.
2. An orange-red color shows that the urine contains glucose. The test result indicates that the person may be a diabetic and should see a doctor for further testing.

## Think and Explore

1. Why is glucose so important to the health of a person?
2. Find out what a person cannot do when the blood glucose is low.
3. Can a diabetic person eat a lot of sugar to overcome the low-glucose problem? Explain your answer.
4. In your opinion, which is a better urine test for glucose, the Benedict's test or the Clinitest pill test? Explain.

# Chapter 8

# The Hormonal System

**Key Terms**
- adrenaline
- catalyst
- distilled water
- hormone
- insulin
- thermostat

The room temperature of many modern homes is regulated by a control system called a thermostat. The thermostat turns on the furnace when the room is cold. Warm air is then blown into the room. On the other hand, when the room is too warm, the thermostat turns off the furnace. This on-and-off mechanism is a good example of a control system. Without the temperature control system, the house may either be too warm or too cold. Similarly, the many activities in your body will not work properly without a control system. Your body is under the control of two systems, the hormonal and the nervous. This chapter discusses the hormonal system. The nervous system will be dealt with in the next chapter.

The body hormonal system is made up of a number of hormonal glands. These glands have no apparent connection except through the blood circulatory system. You have hormonal glands under the brain, in front of the windpipe, above the kidneys, below the stomach, and inside the groin area. All these glands secrete one or more chemicals that control many important life activities. These chemicals, which are called hormones, are very specific in what they do. Hormones affect many body activities, including mental and physical growth and sexual maturity.

The growth hormone in the body affects a person's size. A person may grow to be a ten-foot giant because of too much growth hormone. On the other hand, too little growth hormone may cause a person

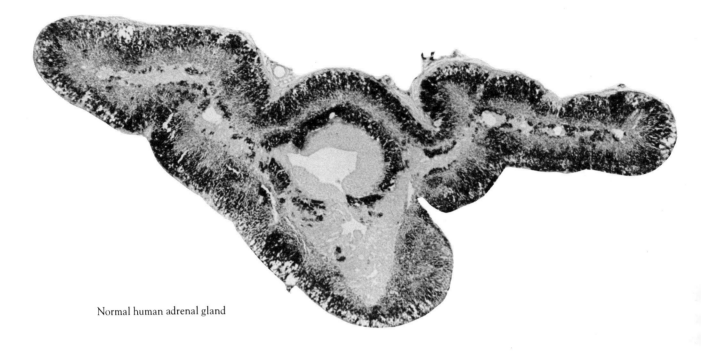

Normal human adrenal gland

to be a three-foot midget. The absence of a hormone called insulin may make a person feel tired and weak all the time. Other hormonal problems may cause a woman to grow a beard or may give a man a high-pitched voice or may make a person unable to handle the stress we all face in living.

A newspaper once reported that a mother had lifted up a car with her bare hands to free her child from underneath it. Something like that does not happen every day. However, it is sometimes possible with the help of a hormone called adrenaline. Adrenaline is released inside you when you feel angry, afraid, or excited. Your heart beats faster and harder. As this continues, more energy is carried to the body cells through the rapidly pumped bloodstream. Obviously body cells that are charged with more energy are prepared to do harder work. And so the woman in the newspaper story had the energy and strength to lift the car.

Even today, the actions of many hormones are not completely known. For one thing the amount of hormone secreted is very small; therefore, it is hard to measure. Hormones work differently from other body activities. Some work very quickly (adrenaline works in seconds). Others work very slowly (growth hormone works over a period of years). One way to help keep the hormonal system healthy is to eat a balanced diet. In most cases a person with a hormonal problem is born with it. Thanks to the marvel of modern science and technology, many hormonal defects can now be corrected with medicine.

## Facts
- Hormones are made mostly of protein and fat— basically the food you eat.
- Hormones can either speed up or slow down a life process (for example, growth).
- The pituitary gland, a hormonal gland under the brain, is about the size of a small pea. The pituitary gland affects most of the other glands in the body. It is sometimes called the master gland.
- Hormones are powerful chemicals. A tiny amount can cause a big change. For example, a woman in her lifetime produces only about a teaspoonful of the female sex hormone.
- Saint Bernards, Great Danes, and several toy-dog breeds are the result of unusual hormone production.

## What Regulates Temperature?

> **Do this activity under the supervision of an adult.**

### Materials
None needed. This activity assumes that the house has a central air-conditioning system, with a furnace and an air conditioner.

### Procedures
1. Find the thermostat in the house. It is a round or rectangular dial on the wall.
2. Examine the thermostat dial carefully to locate the switches (*heat, cool, auto*) and the temperature scales (60, 70, 80, etc.). The switch should be on *heat* in the cold seasons and *cool* in the hot seasons. The heat and cool settings control the furnace for warm air and the air conditioner for cool air.
3. a. Make the thermostat setting at least 5 degrees warmer if you are doing this activity in the cold seasons.
   b. Make the thermostat setting at least 5 degrees cooler if you are doing this activity in the hot seasons.
4. Sit by an air vent and record your observations.

### Conclusions
1. The higher thermostat setting turns on the furnace. The furnace turns off automatically when the air in the room reaches the temperature you chose.

2. The lower thermostat setting turns on the air conditioner to blow cold air. The air conditioner turns off automatically when the air in the room reaches the temperature you chose.
3. In both thermostat settings, it takes time to reach the set temperature.

## Think and Explore
1. Try to think of another example to explain system control or regulation.
2. Is it possible to turn on the furnace and air conditioner at the same time to regulate room temperature? Why?
3. Body temperature for most people is usually 98.6° F (37° C). How does your body keep this same temperature all the time?
4. What happens if your body fails to keep the same temperature all the time?
5. How would you compare keeping the same room temperature and keeping the same body temperature?

## How Can You Control the Mysterious Diver?

### Materials
tall glass cylinder
water
medicine dropper
balloon

### Procedure
1. Fill the glass cylinder to the rim with water.
2. Draw some water into a medicine dropper. Put the dropper in the cylinder.
3. Blow up a balloon. Place the balloon on top of the cylinder.
4. Put your hand on top of the balloon. Press the balloon to make the medicine dropper stay suspended in (a) the top, (b) the middle, and (c) the bottom of the cylinder. It may take several trials before you can place the dropper where you want it to float.

### Conclusions
1. Pressing hard on the balloon makes the dropper stay at the bottom.
2. Pressing lightly makes the dropper stay at the top.
3. Medium pressure keeps the dropper suspended in the middle of the cylinder.

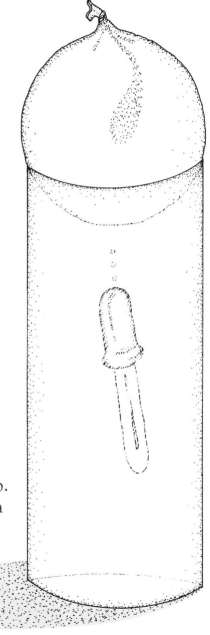

## Think and Explore

1. What must you regulate to keep the medicine dropper in the middle of the cylinder?
2. How will the medicine dropper behave if oil instead of water is put in the glass cylinder?
3. How does the medicine dropper behave when you change the amount of water drawn into it?
4. What comparison do you see between controlling the medicine dropper in the cylinder and controlling life activities in your body?
5. What are some of the problems you would expect if there were no regulation in your body?

## *How Can a Chemical Change the Speed of a Reaction?*

> **Do this activity under the supervision of an adult.**

## Materials
weighing scale
Rochelle salt (sodium potassium tartrate tetrahydrate)
distilled water
measuring cylinder
6% hydrogen peroxide solution
beaker
hot plate
cobalt chloride

## Procedure
1. Weigh 5 grams of Rochelle salt.
2. Dissolve the salt in 5 milliliters of distilled water.
3. Mix the prepared salt solution with 20 milliliters of 6% hydrogen peroxide solution.

4. Warm the solution in a beaker to about 158° F (70° C).
5. Record what happens for about one minute.
6. Add cobalt chloride solution (about 0.2 grams cobalt chloride dissolved in 5 milliliters of distilled water) to the heated salt solution in the beaker.
7. Observe and record.

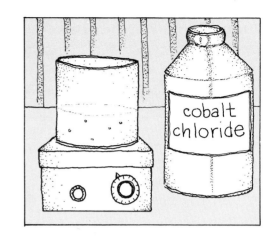

## Conclusions

1. A gas (carbon dioxide) is produced by heating the Rochelle salt solution in the beaker. This gas is produced very slowly, as can be seen by the number of gas bubbles.
2. The gas is produced much more rapidly after the cobalt chloride solution is added. A substance that changes the speed of a reaction is called a catalyst. In this activity the catalyst is cobalt chloride. In similar ways hormones work like catalysts. They change the speed of many body activities.

## Think and Explore

1. How does a catalyst such as cobalt chloride change a chemical reaction?
2. Why are hormones (which act as catalysts) important to your body?
3. What differences, if any, do you see between the work of a catalyst in the laboratory and the work of hormones in your body?
4. How do hormones work in your body over a short period of time? A long period of time?

# Chapter 9

# The Nervous System

When you see a car speeding down the road as you are crossing, you step back and let the car pass. This seemingly simple event involves several body parts working together: your eyes to see the car, your brain to tell you that the car is coming, and your muscles to move the legs. These things have to happen in the correct order if you are to keep from being struck by the car. When a football player reaches up to catch a ball, both hands must work together, or coordinate. If one hand closes and the other does not, then the hands are not coordinated. The player will probably drop the ball. You do many things every day that require coordination. These coordinated activities include getting up in the morning, learning in school, playing in the park, eating dinner, and going to bed. All these activities are coordinated by a very important system of the body—the nervous system.

The nervous system in your body takes the form of a brain and a network of nerves. The largest nerve connected to the brain is the spinal cord. The spinal cord is protected by the backbone. Hundreds of nerves, like wires, branch out from the spinal cord to the body to form a communication network. Each nerve is the pathway by which messages are sent to the brain in answer to a stimulus.

A stimulus is something that causes the whole body or part of the body to act. Usually a stimulus causes a nerve message to be sent to the brain. As a control center, the brain interprets the message and sends another message to tell the body to respond properly to the stimulus. The amount of time it takes the body to respond is the reaction time.

Sometimes the body can respond to a stimulus before the nerve message reaches the brain. Have you ever had the experience of pulling your fingers from a hot object before you knew that it was hot? This is a good example of a reflex action, the simplest type of inborn response in the nervous system. Other examples of reflex actions are sneezing, coughing, blinking the eyes, and jumping when frightened suddenly. Reflex actions are automatic; they are involuntary.

The brain is the headquarters of the whole nervous system. Although the brain works as one unit, it has three parts. Each part controls a different level of activity. The three parts of the brain are the forebrain, the hindbrain, and the brain stem. The forebrain controls movement, sensations, intelligence, and learning. The hindbrain controls muscles and balance. The brain stem controls what might be called the housekeeping jobs of the body—breathing, digestion, and heartbeat.

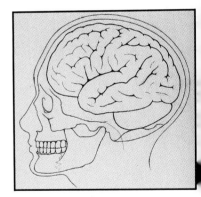

Brain inside human skull

What we know about our surroundings depends on what we know through sight, hearing, taste, smell, and touch. The eyes, ears, tongue, nose, and skin are the special organs of the nervous system. All these sense organs are only receivers of stimuli. The organs themselves cannot make distinctions between bright or dim light, loud or soft noise, or sweet or sour taste; but the brain can. In other words, you literally see, hear, taste, smell, and touch with your brain. Your sense organs cannot be replaced and should be well taken care of. You should see your doctor immediately if the organs are injured or infected.

## Facts

- Your nervous system contains more than 10 billion nerve cells.
- A human nerve message can travel at a rate between 1.6 feet (0.5 meters) per second and 328 feet (100 meters) per second.
- The size of the brain is related to learning and other brain activities. For that reason some people compare brain size with intelligence.
- The human eye is able to see nearly 8 million shades of color.
- People with blue eyes are very sensitive to light.
- Most human beings are able to distinguish 4,000 different scents.

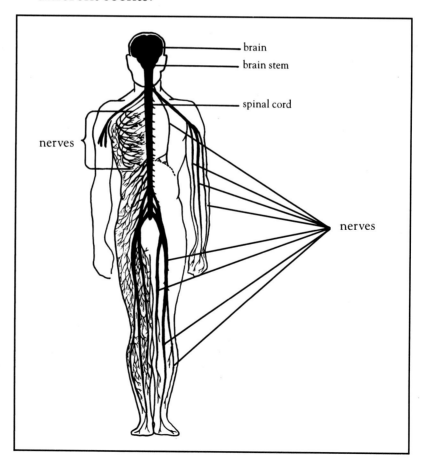

# What Is Your Reaction Time?

## Materials
meter stick
notebook paper

## Procedure

Do this activity with a partner.

1. Rest your arm on a tabletop, with the hand hanging over the edge.
2. Ask your partner to hold a meter stick above your hand. The zero centimeter mark of the meter stick should be between your thumb and index finger.
3. Your partner is to drop the meter stick without warning. You are to catch it as quickly as you can.
4. Record the distance the meter stick falls before you catch it. After you catch the stick, record that as trial 1 in table 1.

**Table 1 Distances Stick Drops**

| Trial | Distance in Centimeters |
|-------|------------------------|
| 1 | _____ |
| 2 | _____ |
| 3 | _____ |
| 4 | _____ |
| 5 | _____ |

5. Repeat steps 3 and 4 four more times. Determine the average by adding the five trials and dividing the sum by five.

6. Find the distance in table 2 that is closest to your average distance. The time opposite the distance is the reaction time.

## Table 2 Reaction Times

| Distance in cm | Reaction time in seconds | Distance in cm | Reaction time in seconds |
|---|---|---|---|
| 6 | 0.11 | 34 | 0.26 |
| 8 | 0.13 | 36 | 0.27 |
| 10 | 0.14 | 38 | 0.28 |
| 12 | 0.16 | 40 | 0.29 |
| 14 | 0.17 | 42 | 0.29 |
| 16 | 0.18 | 44 | 0.30 |
| 18 | 0.19 | 46 | 0.31 |
| 20 | 0.20 | 48 | 0.31 |
| 22 | 0.21 | 50 | 0.32 |
| 24 | 0.22 | 52 | 0.33 |
| 26 | 0.23 | 54 | 0.33 |
| 28 | 0.24 | 56 | 0.34 |
| 30 | 0.25 | 58 | 0.34 |
| 32 | 0.26 | 60 | 0.35 |

## Conclusions

1. Reaction time varies with the individual. Some people have short reaction times—they react quickly to a stimulus. Other people have long reaction times—they react slowly to a stimulus.
2. In the reaction time activity, the following events must happen before one can catch the meter stick:
   a. The eyes see the meter stick drop.
   b. A message is sent from the eyes to the brain.
   c. The brain sends a message to the fingers telling them to catch the meter stick.
   d. The fingers close and catch the meter stick. The time it takes to complete steps a through d is the reaction time.

## Think and Explore

1. Can you shorten your reaction time by having more practices with the same activity? Explain.
2. Is reaction time related to the intelligence of a person? Can you explain why?
3. How will the reaction time be affected if the same person both drops and catches the meter stick?

## What Are Reflex Actions?

## A. The Eye-Blink Reflex

### Materials
notebook paper
a sheet of clear plastic

### Procedure

Do this activity with a partner.

1. Crush a piece of notebook paper to make a paper ball.
2. Hold up a sheet of clear plastic in front of your face.
3. Have your partner throw the paper ball at your face, and watch to see whether your eyes blink.
4. Have your partner throw the paper ball again. This time try hard not to blink your eyes.

### Conclusion
You blink your eyes every time a paper ball is thrown toward your face. You blink even when you try not to.

# B. The Knee-Jerk Reflex

## Materials
none needed

## Procedure
1. Sit down and cross your right leg over the left leg. Allow the right leg to swing freely.
2. Hit your right leg just below the kneecap, using the side of your hand.
3. Observe what happens.
4. Repeat steps 2 and 3 several times.

## Conclusion
The right leg jerks forward.

# C. The Pupil Reflex

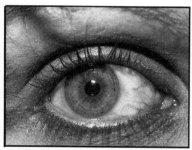

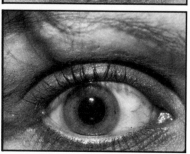

Normal pupil (top)
and dilated pupil (above)

## Materials
mirror
flashlight

## Procedure
1. Look into the mirror. Watch closely the round opening called the pupil. The pupil is surrounded by the colored part (iris) of the eye.
2. Shine a light directly into the pupil and observe any changes.
3. Turn off the light and observe any changes in the pupil.

## Conclusion
The pupil gets smaller when the light is turned on.
The pupil gets bigger after the light is turned off.

## Think and Explore

1. What are the major purposes of reflex actions such as eye-blink, knee-jerk, and pupil reflexes?
2. When dust gets in your eyes, they tear and your eyelids flutter. How does this kind of reflex action protect you?
3. How can you learn to do a reflex action?
4. Can you modify or change a reflex action? Explain your answer.
5. Coughing is a reflex action. Tying shoelaces is a habit. What are the differences between a reflex action and a habit?
6. Explain to another person how you tie a pair of shoelaces. How good is your description? Explain.
7. How can you test whether or not a human behavior is a reflex action?
8. Identify several important characteristics of any reflex action.

## How Good Are Your Senses of Taste and Smell?

### Materials
apple        blindfold
potato       paper cups
pear

### Procedure

Do this activity with a partner.

1. Prepare 9 slices of apple, 9 slices of potato, and 9 slices of pear.
2. Blindfold your partner.

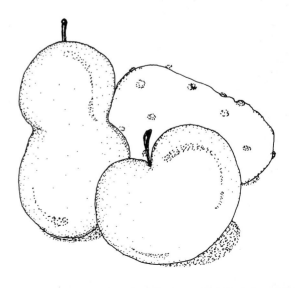

3. Feed your partner a slice of apple, potato, and pear in mixed order. Have him or her rinse the mouth with water between food samples. Your partner is to identify each food immediately after tasting it.
4. Record the results in table 1, using a plus ( + ) for each correct answer and minus ( − ) for each wrong answer.

## Table 1 Identifying by Taste and Smell

| Food | Identification |
|---|---|
| apple | _____ |
| potato | _____ |
| pear | _____ |

5. Repeat step 3. Give your friend the food sample, at the same time holding another food sample under his or her nose. For example, ask your partner to taste a piece of apple while you hold a slice of pear under his or her nose.
6. Record the results in table 2.

## Table 2 Confusing by Added Smell

| Food | Identification |
|---|---|
| apple | _____ |
| potato | _____ |
| pear | _____ |

7. Repeat step 3. This time have your partner taste each of the food samples while holding his or her nose firmly closed.
8. Record the results in table 3.

## Table 3 Blocking the Sense of Smell

| Food | Identification |
|------|----------------|
| apple | ———— |
| potato | ———— |
| pear | ———— |

9. Compare the results in tables 1, 2, and 3.

## Conclusions
Table 1 shows more correct identifications than tables 2 and 3. The identification of food samples in table 1 depends upon the senses of both taste and smell. The sense of taste is confused by the sense of smell in table 2. Finally, the identification in table 3 is made by taste alone without the sense of smell.

## Think and Explore
1. Can the sense of taste or smell be tricked? Explain.
2. Is what we commonly refer to as taste really taste? Explain your answer.
3. How does food taste when you have a burned tongue or a stuffy nose?
4. Which is more powerful, the sense of taste or the sense of smell?
5. What are some of the purposes of taste and smell?
6. What is it about food that is most important to you: (a) its color and texture, (b) its taste, or (c) its smell? Do you know why?

# Can Trial and Error Improve Your Learning?

## Materials
a picture jigsaw puzzle with no more than 20 pieces
clock or watch with a second hand

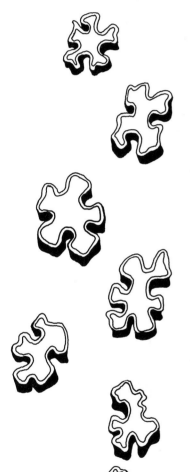

## Procedure
1. Check the time you start. Put the pieces of the jigsaw puzzle together.
2. Record the time it takes you to complete the puzzle.
3. Mix up the pieces and put the puzzle together again.
4. Repeat step 3 twice more. These will be as trials 3 and 4.
5. Record the results in table 1.

## Table 1 Puzzle Trials

| Trial | Time |
|-------|------|
| 1 | ___ |
| 2 | ___ |
| 3 | ___ |
| 4 | ___ |

## Conclusion
Trial 1 takes the longest time. Trial 4 should take the shortest time.

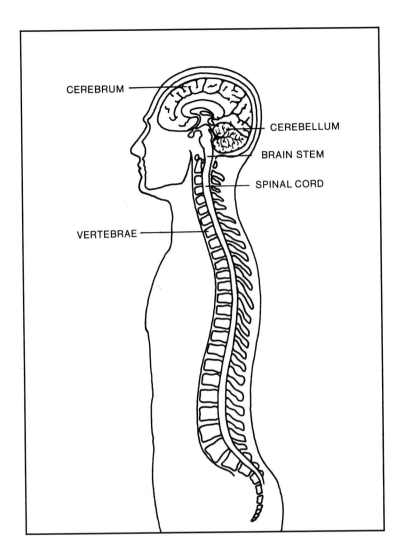

## Think and Explore

1. What is the time difference between trial 1 and trial 4?
2. What causes the time difference?
3. Which trial is trial-and-error learning? How do you know?
4. In which trial did you use memorization to help you complete the puzzle?
5. Did you use trial and error to answer the questions? Explain.

# Chapter 10

# The Reproductive System

**Key Terms**
- egg
- extinct
- generation
- genes
- sex
- sperm
- trait

Look at your family. Do you have brothers, sisters, parents, and grandparents? Have you ever thought how members of the family relate to one another? Members of the family represent human beings from different periods of time called generations. Each member of one generation comes from members of the previous generation. In other words, you come from your parents and your parents come from their parents, whom you call your grandparents. A very important human activity, called reproduction, is involved. Through reproduction human beings are able to produce new human beings. In the case of your family, your grandparents produced your parents and your parents produced you. One day when you get married, you will probably have children. In this way your family continues. Imagine what would happen to your family if they could not reproduce. Family members would not die right away; however, they would die eventually of old age or sickness. In a few generations your family would die out. Now think about this in terms of the whole human race.

The basic design of human reproduction is a simple one. Human beings are classified into two major groups according to their sex. The two groups are the males (men) and the females (women). In human reproduction, a male and female—that is, two parents—are needed to produce offspring. In the reproductive process, each parent contributes a different sex cell. When the male sex cell, called the sperm, unites with the female sex cell, called the egg, a new cell is created. This new cell grows and develops, and a new human life comes into being. The development of the human embryo inside the mother's womb takes about nine months. During this time the different body systems are formed. At the end of the ninth month, the baby is ready to be born. The development of the baby continues for another fifteen to eighteen years until that person becomes a full-grown man or woman.

People around you, including members of your family, are different. They look different and their behavior is also different. What accounts for all these differences? There is no simple answer to the question. However, scientists know that what you are is given to you by your parents. There are special carriers of traits that are built into the sperm and the egg. These carriers are called genes. During the course of reproduction, the genes are combined in different ways to determine the sex, look, and behavior of a person.

## Facts
- A mature woman produces an egg approximately every 28 days.
- It takes about 280 days for a baby to be fully developed and ready to be born.
- Identical twin babies come from the splitting of a fertilized egg, and they are always the same sex.
- The covering system and the nervous system both develop from the same group of cells.
- The lungs of a baby do not begin working until the baby is born.

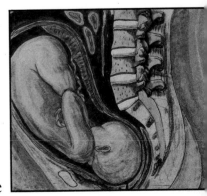

Full term fetus in womb

# How Do Flowering Plants Reproduce?

## Materials
flowers, such as gladioli
safety razor blade
magnifying lens
notebook paper
clear adhesive tape

## Procedure
1. Look at the flower. Find the petals, which are the colored parts of the flower.
2. Pull off all the petals to find a core of stalks in the center of the flower.
3. Find the largest stalk in the core. It is surrounded by several smaller stalks. The big stalk is the pistil; the smaller stalks are the stamens.
4. Remove the stamens and save them for step 8.
5. Remove the pistil. It is the only stalk left in the center of the flower.
6. Slice the base of the pistil in half. The base of the pistil is usually larger than the top.
7. Record what you find inside the base of the pistil.
8. Examine the tip of a stamen with a magnifying lens. What do you see?
9. Tape the pistil and the stamen onto a piece of notebook paper.

## Conclusions

1. At the base of the pistil are some round structures attached to the wall. These round structures are the eggs of the flower. The pistil with the eggs is the female reproductive organ of the flower.
2. Tiny specks are found at the tip of the stamen. These specks are the pollen grains. The grains are the sperm of the flower. The stamen with the pollen grains is the male reproductive organ of the flowering plant.

## Think and Explore

1. For a baby plant to develop, a male pollen grain and a female egg have to come together. This process is called sexual reproduction. How do the pollen grains from the stamen unite with the eggs in the pistil?
2. The flower in the activity has both the male and female reproductive organs. Can you name other plants or animals that have the same setup within their reproductive systems?
3. Compare flower reproduction to human reproduction by listing a few things that they have in common.

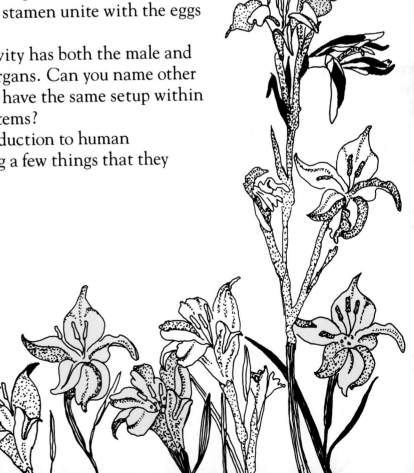

# Where Do Chickens Come From?

**Do this activity under the supervision of an adult.**

## Materials
cardboard box
light bulb
thermometer
shallow dish
timer
12 fertile chicken eggs (obtain from an egg farm or
   hatchery)

## Procedure
1. Build an egg incubator, as shown in the diagram.
2. Maintain a constant temperature of 98.6° F (37° C), controlling the light bulb with the timer. Place a shallow dish of water in the incubator to keep a uniform level of moisture.
3. Put the eggs in the incubator. It is easier if you first put the eggs in an egg carton.
4. Incubate the eggs.
5. Open one egg each day after the third day. Pour the contents into a shallow dish or bowl to see the development of the egg.
6. Stop opening eggs when you see that the contents of an egg are in the form of a small chicken.
7. Wait a few more days. If you are lucky, you may see some wet little chicks work their way out.

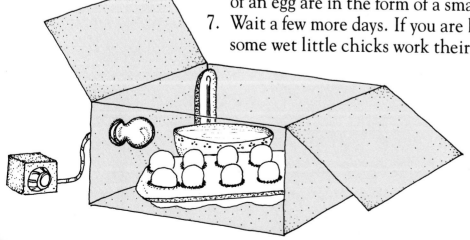

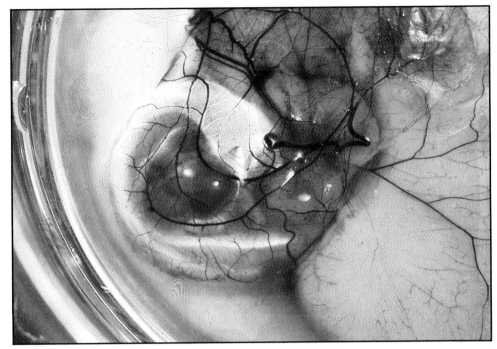

Chick embryo
inside the egg

## Conclusion

The activity shows the development of the chicken
embryo, including the following:

- beating heart
- eyes
- blood vessels
- wing, leg, tail, beak
- sac enclosing embryo
- sac enclosing wastes

## Think and Explore

1. An egg from the supermarket will not hatch into a
   baby chicken. Why do you think this is so?
2. How does the baby chicken obtain food and air
   from inside the egg?
3. How many days will it take a chicken to hatch
   from an egg?
4. Why does it take a human longer to develop than it
   takes a chicken?
5. How does a human baby obtain food and air from
   inside the mother's womb?

# Is It a Boy or a Girl?

## Materials
envelopes
index cards
notebook paper
pencil

## Procedure
1. Prepare two envelopes. Label one envelope "mother" and the other "father."
2. Put twenty cards marked X in the mother envelope. The X represents the sex gene in the mother's egg that helps determine what sex the child will be.
3. Label ten cards with X and ten cards with Y. Mix the cards and put them in the father envelope. The Xs and Ys represent the sex gene of the father's sperm.
4. With your eyes closed, pull one card from the mother envelope and one card from the father envelope.
5. If both cards are marked X, put a check mark under XX in the following table. If one card has X and other Y, put the check mark under XY.

| XX | XY |
|----|----|
| ———— | ———— |
| ———— | ———— |
| ———— | ———— |
| ———— | ———— |
| ———— | ———— |

6. Return the cards to the envelopes and repeat steps 4 and 5 twenty-five times. Record the results each time. Then tally the results you got.

## Conclusion

The sex genes (X and Y) determine whether a sperm-egg combination is a boy or a girl. An XX combination results in a girl. An XY combination results in a boy. Your tally of the results you entered in the table gives you the number of boys and girls you get in twenty-five trial combinations.

## Think and Explore

1. There are about an equal number of boys and girls in the world. Why do you think this is so?
2. John wanted a son because he had only daughters. He blamed his wife for this. Was John being fair?
3. Some families have only boys or girls. Can you explain why this happens?
4. Is it possible to determine the sex of a baby before its birth? Explain.

# GLOSSARY OF TERMS

**ABSORPTION**—The taking of digested food into the bloodstream.

**ADRENALINE**—The hormone that speeds up the rate of heartbeat and breathing.

**ALBUMIN**—A rich protein. Albumin is found in egg white and milk.

**ANTI-INVASION FACTOR (AIF)**—A substance found in the soft bone called the cartilage. In laboratory tests, AIF slows down cancer and gum diseases.

**ARTERY**—A blood vessel that carries blood away from the heart.

**BACTERIA**—Simple small living things. Some types carry diseases. Others work for the good of the body.

**BENEDICT'S SOLUTION**—A blue solution for testing sugar.

**BICEPS**—The upper arm muscle. The biceps muscle pulls the forearm toward the shoulder.

**BIURET SOLUTION**—A solution for testing protein.

**BLADDER**—A muscular sac that stores urine.

**BLOOD**—A red fluid that circulates in the blood vessels.

**BRAIN STEM**—The lower part of the brain. The brain stem controls heartbeat, breathing, and other important life activities.

**CALCIUM**—An important chemical found in the bones and teeth. Calcium helps to make the bones and teeth strong.

**CALORIE**—A measurement of energy in food.

**CANCER**—An abnormal condition in which cells divide rapidly with no control. Cancer can affect many parts of the body, such as the skin, lungs, mouth, and nose.

**CAPILLARY**—A tiny blood vessel. In the capillaries, food and wastes exchange between the blood and the surrounding cells.

**CARBOHYDRATE**—A family of sugar-related substances. Carbohydrates provide the main sources of energy for the body.

**CARBON DIOXIDE**—A gas exhaled by the lungs. The gas is produced by the process of respiration.

**CARTILAGE**—Soft bone. Parts of the nose and ears are made of cartilage.

**CATALYST**—A substance that changes the speed of an activity. Adrenaline is a catalyst that speeds up the rate of the heartbeat.

**CELL**—The basic unit of life. The body is made of many cells.

**CENTIGRADE**—A scale of temperature. Water freezes at zero degrees and boils at one hundred degrees centigrade.

**CONTRACTION OF MUSCLE**—To shorten the length of the muscle.

**CONTROL**—A standard usually used in an experiment for comparison. To find the effect of a drug, for example, person A is given the drug and person B is left without it. The effect of the drug can be identified by comparing person A with person B. Person B in this experiment is the control.

**COORDINATION**—The working together of two or more parts. When both hands come together to catch a ball, the two hands are working in coordination.

**DIABETES**—A disease in which a person has too much sugar in his blood. A person with diabetes that is not treated feels tired and weak.

**DIABETIC**—A person suffering from diabetes.

**DIAPHRAGM**—A large flat muscle on the bottom of the chest cavity. The diaphragm helps breathing by its up-and-down movement.

**DISTILLED WATER**—A pure water made by boiling water into steam and cooling the steam back into water.

**EGG**—A female reproductive cell.

**ESOPHAGUS**—The food tube that connects the stomach to the back of the mouth. The esophagus is a part of the digestive system.

**ETHER**—A light liquid that can easily put people to sleep. Ether is used commonly in the laboratory to put experimental animals to sleep.

**EXTINCT**—Having died out; no longer existing.

**FAT**—A substance in the body important for the storage and production of energy. Fat is found in foods like cream, butter, and meat.

**FECES**—The solid human waste from the digestive system.

**FILTRATION**—The separation of two substances through a filter screen. The separation of sand from water by means of a fine screen is filtration.

**FOREBRAIN**—The largest part of the brain. The forebrain controls activities such as speech, hearing, taste, and smell.

**GENE**—An important part of the cell that carries traits between generations.

**GENERATION**—A time period in the development of a family. The grandparents represent one generation. The parents represent another generation. The children represent a third generation.

**GLUCOSE**—A simple sugar.

**HABIT**—A learned behavior that is done without having to think about it. Buttoning your coat is a habit.

**HINDBRAIN**—The rear part of the brain. The hindbrain controls the muscles and keeps the sense of balance.

**HORMONE**—A chemical that changes the speed of some important body activities. Growth hormone is a chemical that increases the growth of bones.

**INBORN**—Present at birth. Eye blinking is an inborn behavior.

**INDICATOR**—A substance that changes color in the presence of another substance. Phenolphthalein is an indicator that turns colorless in the presence of acids.

**INSULIN**—A chemical that helps to store sugar in the liver.

**INVOLUNTARY**—Acting without the person's control. The beating of the heart is involuntary.

**IODINE SOLUTION**—A solution to test the presence of starch. The solution turns blue-black in starch.

**JOINT**—A place where two bones meet to permit movement. The elbow joint permits the movement of the arm.

**KNEE JERK**—An automatic action in which the leg kicks forward when it is hit just below the kneecap.

**LACTIC ACID**—A weak acid found in sour milk.

**LIVER**—An organ that is under the right side of the diaphragm. The organ has many functions, including digestion.

**LUNG**—The organ of breathing.

**MARROW**—A substance in the bone for producing blood cells.

**MEASUREMENT**—The act of calculating length, area, volume, and weight.

**MEAT GRAIN**—The pattern of the meat fibers.

**MICROSCOPE**—An instrument that helps to make small things look large.

**MUCUS**—A sticky substance made by the body.

**NERVES**—Simple units of the nervous system. The nerves tell the body about its environment.

**NUTRIENTS**—Useful things we get from food.

**ORGAN**—Several cell groups that work together to do a special job. The heart, the lungs, and the kidneys are organs.

**OXYGEN**—A gas in the air that supports life. We need oxygen to live.

**PANCREAS**—An organ that produces digestive juices and hormones.

**PERISTALSIS**—A muscular action that pushes food through the digestive tract.

**PHENOLPHTHALEIN**—A testing fluid for acids and bases.

**PHOSPHORUS**—An important substance in the bones and teeth. Phosphorus shines faintly in the dark and starts to burn when brought out in the air.

**PLAQUE**—A hard substance formed on teeth. Plaque breeds bacteria.

**PROTEIN**—An important chemical in many foods and living things. Protein is important for body building.

**PULSE**—The beat of a large blood vessel as blood is pumped through it. A pulse can be felt on the surface of the skin close to the large blood vessel.

**PUPIL**—A small round opening in the middle of the colored part of the eye.

**RADIAL ARTERY**—A big blood vessel close to the radius bone of the forearm.

**REACTION TIME**—The time it takes to respond to a stimulus. A person who is slow to respond has a long reaction time.

**REFLEX ACTION**—An automatic response that is not learned. The eye blink is a reflex action.

**RELAXATION OF MUSCLE**—To return the muscle to its resting condition. This action is the opposite of muscle contraction.

**RESPONSE**—An answer to some kind of action. For example, drinking water is a response to being thirsty.

**SALIVA**—The liquid that mixes with the food we chew. Saliva comes from the salivary glands of the mouth.

**SALIVARY GLANDS**—A group of special cells in the mouth that make saliva.

**SEX**—The condition of being a female (woman) or a male (man).

**SKELETON**—A frame of bones.

**SPERM**—The male cell of reproduction.

**SPINAL CORD**—A group of nerves inside the backbone. The spinal cord connects to the base of the brain.

**STIMULUS**—Something that makes you act in a certain way.

**SWEAT**—The liquid waste produced by the skin.

**SWEAT GLAND**—A special skin cell that produces a liquid waste called sweat.

**SWEAT PORE**—A very tiny opening on the skin where sweat is produced.

**SYSTEM**— A group of related body parts that work together. The muscles and bones are two systems of the body.

**TENDON**—A strong tissue that connects bones and muscles.

**THERMOSTAT**—An instrument that can be set to keep a certain level of temperature. A thermostat can be found in the house and in the car.

**TRAIT**—A special quality. A tall person's special trait is his or her height.

**TRANSLUCENT**—A condition of letting light through so that objects beyond cannot be seen clearly. A piece of wax paper is translucent.

**TRIAL AND ERROR**—Learning by trying different ways.

**TRICEPS**—A muscle on the underside of the arm. The triceps and biceps muscles work together to bend the forearm.

**URINE**—A liquid waste made by the kidneys.

**VEIN**—A blood vessel that carries blood back to the heart.

**VINEGAR**—A mild acid. Vinegar is used commonly in the kitchen for cooking.

**VITAMIN**—An important chemical to maintain the proper function of many life activities. For example, vitamin D is important for maintaining strong teeth and bones.

**VOCAL CORD**—A tissue in the voice box for making sound.

**VOLUNTARY**—Acting by choice.

# Index

**About the author**

Ovid Wong earned his B.Sc. in biology from the University of Alberta, Edmonton, Canada, his M.Ed. in curriculum from the University of Washington, Seattle, and his Ph.D. in science education from the University of Illinois, Urbana-Champaign. He is currently the science curriculum specialist with school district #65 in Evanston. Since 1984 he has served as a consultant for the Illinois State Board of Education and the State Board of Higher Education.

Dr. Wong's work has appeared on public television and in such journals as the *Science Teacher*, the *American Biology Teacher*, *ISTA Spectrum*, the *Bilingual Journal* and a number of professional newsletters. Dr. Wong is the author of *A Glossary of Biology*. *Your Body and How It Works* is his first book for Childrens Press.